DUNCAN JAMES

OLD JEWELLERY

SHIRE PUBLICATIONS LTD

Cover: (Top left) A Victorian oval mourning brooch, gold with hair, and set with garnets and pearls; c.1870. (Top right) A Victorian brooch, gold with turquoise enamel, and set with coral and pearls. (Below) An early Victorian 'cannetille' gold necklace, set with pink topaz; c.1830. (Below centre) Garnet drop earrings, c.1880.

British Library Cataloguing in Publication Data: James, Duncan. Old Jewellery. 1. Jewellery, history. I. Title. 739.27'09. ISBN 0-7478-0047-2.

Printed in Great Britain by C. I. Thomas & Sons (Haverfordwest) Ltd, Press Buildings, Merlins Bridge, Haverfordwest, Dyfed SA61 1XF.

Contents

Acknowledgements

My warm thanks are due to the many friends who have generously loaned jewellery to me for producing drawings and photographs. I am also indebted to the staff of Messrs Russell, Baldwin and Bright of Leominster for their assistance in the preparation of the cover photograph.

List of illustrations

Introduction

This book is about old jewellery, not ancient jewellery. It seeks to provide information about the sort of brooches, rings, bracelets and earrings that have been handed down through the family, perhaps over two or three generations. Often such pieces are good of their type but, being broken, unfashionable or simply misunderstood, they risk being consigned to the scrap dealer: the great misfortune of precious jewellery is its vulnerability, because in every age it risks being reduced to the simple cash equivalent of its intrinsic value.

If an item of jewellery is worn more than just occasionally, its chance of survival in pristine condition is not high, and daily wear will, within a few decades, convert the finest gem-set gold or platinum ring to a chipped, abraded and fragile wreck. The way in which fine jewellery is treated is a cause of much dismay; there is a misapprehension that because diamonds are the hardest substance known to man they are therefore indestructible and that gold, since it is a noble metal, can resist all manner of mistreatment.

There is also a stubborn insistence that old jewellery should still be worn daily (and often, therefore, damaged) in spite of its antiquity, fragility and beauty. When vintage cars are no longer allowed to suffer the perils of regular use and when fine and valuable china is sensibly retired to the display cabinet, it does seem odd that so many people insist on wearing and jeopardising equally valuable and beautiful objects on the pretext that they are jewels and therefore must be worn.

This book is not intended to be a guide to styles and dates but is an attempt to offer some insight into a fascinating subject. It seeks to encourage the reader to look at jewellery more closely and carefully for the subtle hidden evidence of fine craftsmanship and design. It is written in the belief that a knowledge of the skills used to make jewellery will lead to a greater appreciation of its beauty.

Plate 1. A late Victorian 9 carat red-gold bracelet. The locket clasp is a later addition. There is no hallmark although '9ct' is stamped on various components.

Plate 2. Detail of the Victorian bracelet showing the well rounded D-section profile of the wire. Close inspection of the inside of the links shows that they were made using thin sheet which was rolled in along the edges. (A similar example is shown in figure 6.)

1
Types of jewellery

Jewellery takes many forms and serves a multitude of subtle purposes. It may constitute a display of raw wealth by the exhibition of precious stones and valuable metal, or as a delicate jewel of gold with a few pearls it may be a slight but thoughtful expression of discreet good taste. Much jewellery takes the form of a favoured talisman or symbolic device related to a religious faith or secular interest, and that other passion, love, has always been a major reason for the giving of jewellery. However, above and beyond all this, jewellery has a decorative purpose — it is designed simply to adorn the individual.

Rings

Of the many types of jewellery the finger ring is the most intimate and symbolically charged form. An unbroken circle signifies eternity, so as a token of friendship, love and marriage the simple gold ring has no equal. Unfortunately it is the category of jewellery that is the least likely to survive intact since often a ring is worn constantly until it is either lost or damaged or just disintegrates. One ring may be worn alongside another so that they wear each other away, or repeated size alterations will have damaged the shank or the setting. Thus a good example of any ring that has survived for more than a couple of generations is rare and therefore worth cherishing — preferably by not wearing it.

If a ring breaks it is invariably at one of the solder joints (figure 1). Stone settings and signet-ring tops are often made separately so that a range of shank sizes can be fitted (this is a relatively recent technique). Older wedding bands always have a joint (usually arranged well clear of the assay mark), whereas modern rings are sawn from a length of seamless gold tube.

Because a ring is in close contact with the finger, it has always been important to use one of the noble metals in order to avoid irritating the skin. Good-quality stones tend to be set in a higher carat value of gold, such as 18 carat (not 22 carat, which is too soft), or platinum. Similarly the quality of craftsmanship in a jewel tends to improve as the intrinsic value of the ingredients rises.

A popular ring in Victorian times was one in which the initial letters of a series of stones spelt out a message of affection. Thus the word 'regard' was made using six stones: ruby, emerald,

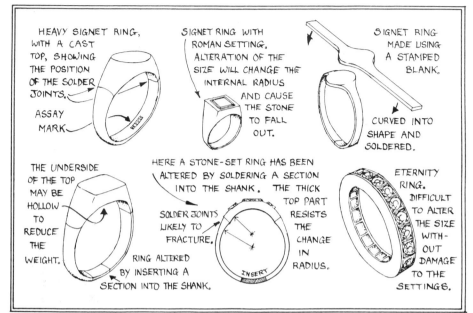

HEAVY SIGNET RING, WITH A CAST TOP, SHOWING THE POSITION OF THE SOLDER JOINTS.

ASSAY MARK

SIGNET RING WITH ROMAN SETTING. ALTERATION OF THE SIZE WILL CHANGE THE INTERNAL RADIUS AND CAUSE THE STONE TO FALL OUT.

SIGNET RING MADE USING A STAMPED BLANK.

CURVED INTO SHAPE AND SOLDERED.

THE UNDERSIDE OF THE TOP MAY BE HOLLOW TO REDUCE THE WEIGHT.

HERE A STONE-SET RING HAS BEEN ALTERED BY SOLDERING A SECTION INTO THE SHANK. THE THICK TOP PART RESISTS THE CHANGE IN RADIUS.

SOLDER JOINTS LIKELY TO FRACTURE.

RING ALTERED BY INSERTING A SECTION INTO THE SHANK.

INSERT

ETERNITY RING. DIFFICULT TO ALTER THE SIZE WITHOUT DAMAGE TO THE SETTINGS.

Figure 1. Rings — a few examples.

garnet, amethyst, ruby and diamond. The result was not aesthetically satisfactory but the arrangement was popular. A further variety was the use of lapis lazuli, opal, verd-antique and emerald to give the message 'love'. Another coded arrangement of stones was the sequence diamond, emerald, amethyst, ruby, emerald, sardonyx (brown/red, similar to cornelian) and topaz, to give the word 'dearest'.

Brooches

The larger scope for design in a brooch makes it an object of great interest. It can be in a sense a miniature picture. It had a practical origin in the cloak fastenings of the Celts, which evolved to become richly ornate and expressive, but for the most part it has lost any practical function in recent times.

Although the greater structural complexity of the brooch does render it vulnerable, it tends not to wear out in the way that a ring or a bracelet will. Often, however, an old brooch can be marred by clumsy repair work to the fittings or a poor replacement for a missing pin. Figure 2 shows a range of designs of brooch pins.

Frequently the brooch will be formed as a hollow structure. This was and is done partly to reduce the cost but also to reduce the weight, because a heavy brooch is damaging to delicate fabrics and tends not to sit well on the material. The fact that an item of jewellery is hollow is usually obvious from the weight, but the presence of tiny breather holes in the back, which allowed soldering to be carried out when the piece was made, will offer proof (see figure 3). Unfortunately, hollow work is very often made using excessively thin metal so it is easily dented or even crushed. There is also a tendency for the metal to tear around the stress points of hinge and latch. Such damage is difficult to repair.

A gem-set brooch may pose a problem if any of the stones are missing since even a well matched replacement can look out of place simply by being new and unscarred. Colour matching is always difficult because most stones have a wide range of colour. In addition there are many idiosyncratic ways in which a gem can be cut and this too can have a marked effect upon the appearance. Old stones may also have suffered colour changes which can make them look totally unlike new material. Turquoise, for instance, ages to an unattractive green, and some stones fade as a result of prolonged exposure to light.

Figure 2. A selection of brooch-pin designs.

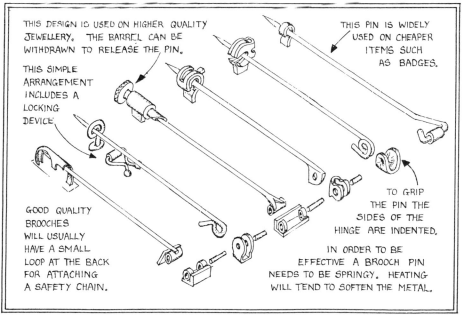

THIS DESIGN IS USED ON HIGHER QUALITY JEWELLERY. THE BARREL CAN BE WITHDRAWN TO RELEASE THE PIN.

THIS SIMPLE ARRANGEMENT INCLUDES A LOCKING DEVICE.

THIS PIN IS WIDELY USED ON CHEAPER ITEMS SUCH AS BADGES.

GOOD QUALITY BROOCHES WILL USUALLY HAVE A SMALL LOOP AT THE BACK FOR ATTACHING A SAFETY CHAIN.

TO GRIP THE PIN THE SIDES OF THE HINGE ARE INDENTED.

IN ORDER TO BE EFFECTIVE A BROOCH PIN NEEDS TO BE SPRINGY. HEATING WILL TEND TO SOFTEN THE METAL.

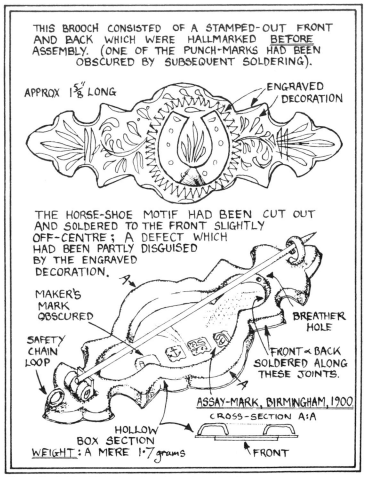

THIS BROOCH CONSISTED OF A STAMPED-OUT FRONT
AND BACK WHICH WERE HALLMARKED <u>BEFORE</u>
ASSEMBLY. (ONE OF THE PUNCH-MARKS HAD BEEN
OBSCURED BY SUBSEQUENT SOLDERING).

APPROX 1⅝" LONG

ENGRAVED
DECORATION

THE HORSE-SHOE MOTIF HAD BEEN CUT OUT
AND SOLDERED TO THE FRONT SLIGHTLY
OFF-CENTRE; A DEFECT WHICH
HAD BEEN PARTLY DISGUISED
BY THE ENGRAVED
DECORATION.

MAKER'S
MARK
OBSCURED

SAFETY
CHAIN
LOOP

BREATHER
HOLE

FRONT & BACK
SOLDERED ALONG
THESE JOINTS.

ASSAY-MARK, BIRMINGHAM, 1900.

CROSS-SECTION A:A

HOLLOW
BOX SECTION
<u>WEIGHT</u>: A MERE 1·7 grams

FRONT

Figure 3. A late Victorian silver brooch in detail.

Much use was made by the Victorians of organic substances such as hair and butterfly wings. Brooches were often made to serve as mourning jewellery with provision for a beautifully arranged lock of hair to be held behind crystal, either displayed at the front or discreetly hidden at the back. These easily became damaged by damp, or the hair was removed because with a change in fashion it came to be regarded as morbid. Butterfly wings are also subject to damage by moisture.

Scottish brooches using cairngorms (citrine) and agates seldom

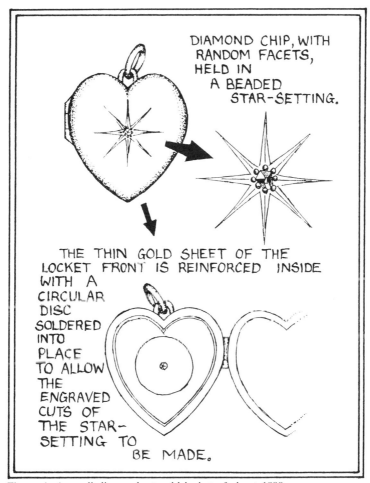

DIAMOND CHIP, WITH RANDOM FACETS, HELD IN A BEADED STAR-SETTING.

THE THIN GOLD SHEET OF THE LOCKET FRONT IS REINFORCED INSIDE WITH A CIRCULAR DISC SOLDERED INTO PLACE TO ALLOW THE ENGRAVED CUTS OF THE STAR-SETTING TO BE MADE.

Figure 4. A small diamond-set gold locket of about 1890.

use standard cuts. Often the specially shaped stones are held in place with a form of glue or cement which softens with heat, and once lost they are almost impossible to replace.

Engraving is a feature of much old jewellery, including brooches (see figure 3). The quality of workmanship varies enormously and it is worth looking closely, with an eyeglass, in order to judge the artistic sensitivity of the engraver. Sometimes the cutting is deep enough seriously to weaken the metal and cracks can develop within a pattern of heavy decoration.

Shell cameos set in gold were invariably of good quality and even those with pinchbeck frames would today be considered good. Pinchbeck, a type of brass with a good gold colour, was often assembled using lead solder, which is soft, so these frames are usually falling apart. Since the designs can be pleasantly extravagant they deserve careful repair. Cameos may also be found carved in ivory, jet, various colours of lava, onyx, sardonyx or haematite, and also made in porcelain.

Lockets

Because of the need for an accurately fitted hinge, the locket has always been a more difficult object to manufacture and was therefore often the product of a specialist workshop (figure 4). Frequently only the front and back were made of gold (or rolled gold), the rest being formed from brass. Engraving was widely used for applying decoration.

The locket was sometimes part of a parure (see below, under Necklaces). Examples used to mourn a loved one were decorated with black enamel or made in jet or vulcanite. In addition to a photograph, a lock of hair was often carried inside.

Figure 5. A close look at four different types of chain.

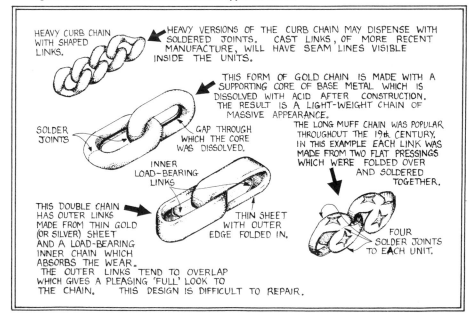

HEAVY CURB CHAIN WITH SHAPED LINKS.

HEAVY VERSIONS OF THE CURB CHAIN MAY DISPENSE WITH SOLDERED JOINTS. CAST LINKS, OF MORE RECENT MANUFACTURE, WILL HAVE SEAM LINES VISIBLE INSIDE THE UNITS.

THIS FORM OF GOLD CHAIN IS MADE WITH A SUPPORTING CORE OF BASE METAL WHICH IS DISSOLVED WITH ACID AFTER CONSTRUCTION. THE RESULT IS A LIGHT-WEIGHT CHAIN OF MASSIVE APPEARANCE.

SOLDER JOINTS

GAP THROUGH WHICH THE CORE WAS DISSOLVED.

INNER LOAD-BEARING LINKS

THE LONG MUFF CHAIN WAS POPULAR THROUGHOUT THE 19th CENTURY. IN THIS EXAMPLE EACH LINK WAS MADE FROM TWO FLAT PRESSINGS WHICH WERE FOLDED OVER AND SOLDERED TOGETHER.

THIS DOUBLE CHAIN HAS OUTER LINKS MADE FROM THIN GOLD (OR SILVER) SHEET AND A LOAD-BEARING INNER CHAIN WHICH ABSORBS THE WEAR. THE OUTER LINKS TEND TO OVERLAP WHICH GIVES A PLEASING 'FULL' LOOK TO THE CHAIN. THIS DESIGN IS DIFFICULT TO REPAIR.

THIN SHEET WITH OUTER EDGE FOLDED IN.

FOUR SOLDER JOINTS TO EACH UNIT.

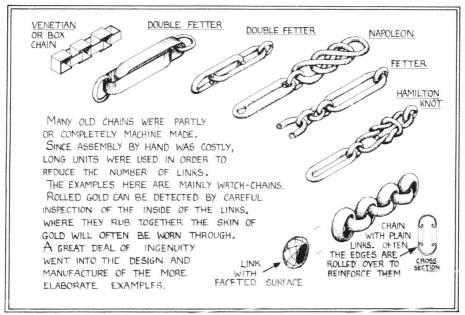

Figure 6. A small selection of late Victorian chains.

Chains

Whereas modern silver and gold chains are made by machine, for much of the nineteenth century chains had to be fashioned laboriously, using hand-working skills. With this limitation in mind the craftsmen avoided very fine links, and chains were evidently designed carefully in order to reduce the time needed to make them. Thus one can find that long units were used in order to reduce the number of links (figure 6), and some chains were cunningly made from hundreds of tiny stampings which needed no soldering.

The *graduated curb chain,* in which the thickness of the wire, as well as the diameter of the links, was arranged to increase towards the centre, is a typical example of labour-intensive chainmaking.

The *loop-in-loop chain,* which is of ancient origin, had the advantage that the individual loops could be soldered before assembly, thus avoiding the risk of accidentally 'flooding' a number of links with solder and so locking them together. There are many clever variations on this simple basic idea.

The *watch-chain* is the prominent example of the use of chain

Plate 3. A silver watch-chain of fancy design, with five hollow beads and a tassel (about 1870). This type was also known as a leontine. Two types of chain are used: loop-in-loop and a heavy trace chain.

in jewellery and it served the significant practical function of allowing the watch to be hauled from the pocket and retained securely while in use. Figure 6 shows a few of the more fancy designs. The *albert* was a long chain which was secured at the centre to one of the buttonholes of the waistcoat and hung in curves to pockets on each side. One end was fixed to the watch whilst the other, typically, was attached to a seal or fob of some sort. A *half albert,* as the name suggests, was a shorter chain that hung on one side only. The *leontine* was also a short watch chain but of a more decorative form for use on special occasions. Although countless different designs were used, the *curb chain* is probably the most familiar.

Chains carved from jet or moulded in vulcanite were worn when a family was in mourning.

Long chains were also worn; known as *guard chains,* these were used to secure such items as watches, keys and lorgnettes. The *muff chain* served a similar function. Figure 5 shows a typical design.

Necklaces

'Necklace' is a general term which covers many types of jewellery designed to be worn at the neck. The more elaborate forms might well include gemstones, either oval or pear-shaped, in a centred arrangement of three, five or seven. Often a necklace will form part of a suite of jewels including a pair of bracelets, a pair of earrings and a brooch or tiara, the entire ensemble having its own fitted and lined box. Such a set is known as a *parure* and a smaller set, of perhaps only two items that match, is a *demi-parure*. Jewellery of this form is often designed so that it may be dismantled and worn as a different arrangement or so that parts of it may be used separately.

Earrings

Often only one of a pair of earrings survives or some damaging alterations have been made to meet a change of fashion. Victorian earrings were, after about 1865, worn long and these tend to have suffered through being shortened.

An ear pendant with three or more drops is known as a *girandole*. Weight has always been an important consideration in

Plate 4. A heavy silver graduated half albert watch-chain; weight 43 grams (approximately 1.3 ounces troy); hallmarked Chester 1913. Each link is marked with the lion passant (sterling), and the main marks are on the largest central link. This is a curb chain as shown in figure 5.

Plate 5. A nineteenth-century necklace with large amethysts set in simple collets of silver. The stones in this example were well matched and attractive but not of the highest quality, since the colour was rather uneven.

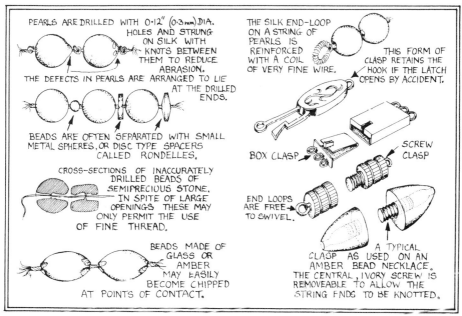

Figure 7. Beads, pearls and clasps.

the manufacture of earrings, so large designs are usually hollow, thin or made of a light material. Hollow pieces are naturally vulnerable and any dents which they acquire are usually impossible to remove.

Any ear pendant will suffer a large amount of wear on the suspension links because of the constant movement of the head, and the heavier the pendant the greater the wear.

Bracelets

At its simplest a bracelet is a chain with a clasp, at its most complex a gem-set concoction of decorated units hinged together. (See figure 52 for a bracelet set with gems.) It may be a bangle with a rolled-on decoration or a hollow hinged type in two sections. All will have one thing in common, if worn frequently: they will have suffered a great deal of damage. Hollow bangles always become dented, and linked or hinged units will have worn thin at points of contact. Heavy bracelets suffer more from this type of damage.

A typical bracelet has a straight length of 190mm (7½ inches) but wrist sizes vary considerably, so this is only a guide. To be comfortable, the bracelet should accommodate itself to the oval shape of the wrist and not fall too far down on the hand. It can be pleasant to feel a bracelet moving on the arm rather than wearing it clamped tightly to the flesh.

The *charm bracelet* with its jangling festoon of battered objects is not to everyone's taste but the older and better made miniature charms, if they are not worn to oblivion, can be fascinating things to study. Modern charms (post-1940s) may be castings, which are often poorly finished.

The *gate bracelet* in its many forms has a long history and good Victorian examples, often made in red gold, do survive.

Cufflinks

Cufflinks came into use during the nineteenth century and were often made in a utilitarian form, being little more than linked buttons. Sometimes the decoration was on one link only. Modern cufflinks are made with a swivel mechanism, whilst older designs usually have a simple chain connecting the two parts.

If the design includes precise or geometric patterning this will have been carried out using machine engraving.

Tiepins

Tiepins were very widely used to anchor the tie to the shirt front and they gave the wearer a chance to display his interests, his good taste or, in a discreet way, his wealth. Made in a huge variety of designs, they were usually fitted with a long pin, which was grooved to help hold it in the fabric.

Beads

Since beads are usually strung on cotton or silk they are always vulnerable to losses, and bead necklaces of any antiquity are seldom complete. Spacers may be used to reduce chafing and damage to adjacent beads, or the string itself may include knots for the same reason (figure 7).

Beads of natural material such as agate or garnet are often crudely drilled, first from one side, then from the other. These holes seldom meet accurately in the middle, so an apparently large opening will often admit only a narrow string (or a thin filament of nylon).

2
The principal decorative techniques

There are a number of well established techniques, mostly of ancient origin, that can be found in every category of old jewellery and deserve special mention in order that they may be easily identified. Methods for using the metal itself to form the decoration are dealt with first.

Repoussé

Repoussé is a method of imparting a raised design or pattern to a flat sheet of metal by punching the forms in from the back. This is achieved by supporting the metal on a block of pitch, which provides a resilient 'cushion', and forming areas which have to be raised by the careful use of a series of punches with rounded tips (figure 8).

Not all of the detailed work can be introduced in this way, so the metal is turned over and the finer features of the design are punched in from the front, once again with the pitch providing

Figure 8. Tools for repoussé work.

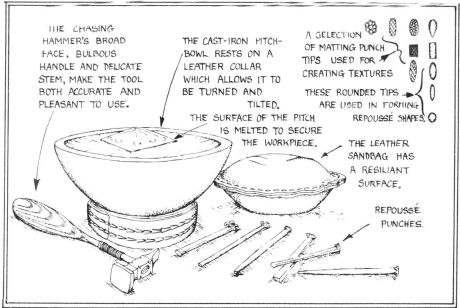

THE CHASING HAMMER'S BROAD FACE, BULBOUS HANDLE AND DELICATE STEM, MAKE THE TOOL BOTH ACCURATE AND PLEASANT TO USE.

THE CAST-IRON PITCH-BOWL RESTS ON A LEATHER COLLAR WHICH ALLOWS IT TO BE TURNED AND TILTED. THE SURFACE OF THE PITCH IS MELTED TO SECURE THE WORKPIECE.

A SELECTION OF MATTING PUNCH TIPS USED FOR CREATING TEXTURES

THESE ROUNDED TIPS ARE USED IN FORMING REPOUSSÉ SHAPES.

THE LEATHER SANDBAG HAS A RESILIANT SURFACE.

REPOUSSÉ PUNCHES.

the support. The use of steel punches in this way is called *chasing*. As with repoussé, the guiding principle is that of pushing the metal into shape. Because repoussé techniques are time-consuming they tend to have been used in Western jewellery only for the larger, more valuable pieces. In countries where labour costs are low, repoussé work may be produced because it is one way of creating large and impressive items of jewellery whilst keeping the outlay on precious metal as low as possible.

Stamping

Many pieces of old jewellery can be found which, although they may appear to have been made by repoussé methods, have been the subject of a production technique which involved stamping the metal into shape between a steel punch and a die (figure 9). Indications that such a method has been used are the very crisp detail, often on the back as well as the front, and the use of thin sheet of an even thickness. The quality of such work lies in the artistic merit of the design and with the skill of the craftsman who had the difficult job of cutting the dies.

There are many secondary techniques used in the shaping of

Figure 9. Dies and punches.

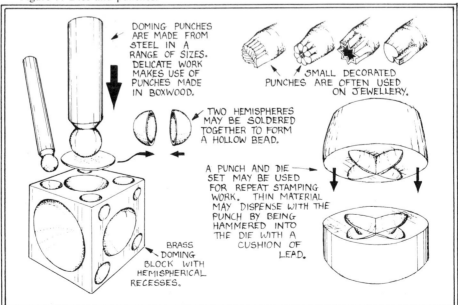

DOMING PUNCHES ARE MADE FROM STEEL IN A RANGE OF SIZES. DELICATE WORK MAKES USE OF PUNCHES MADE IN BOXWOOD.

SMALL DECORATED PUNCHES ARE OFTEN USED ON JEWELLERY.

TWO HEMISPHERES MAY BE SOLDERED TOGETHER TO FORM A HOLLOW BEAD.

A PUNCH AND DIE SET MAY BE USED FOR REPEAT STAMPING WORK. THIN MATERIAL MAY DISPENSE WITH THE PUNCH BY BEING HAMMERED INTO THE DIE WITH A CUSHION OF LEAD.

BRASS DOMING BLOCK WITH HEMISPHERICAL RECESSES.

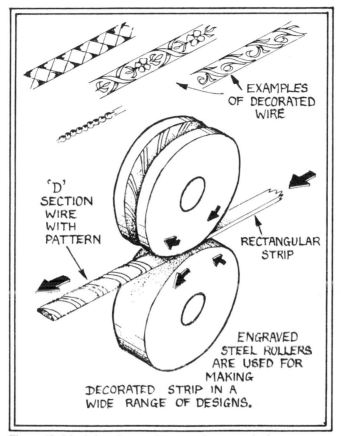

EXAMPLES OF DECORATED WIRE

'D' SECTION WIRE WITH PATTERN

RECTANGULAR STRIP

ENGRAVED STEEL ROLLERS ARE USED FOR MAKING DECORATED STRIP IN A WIDE RANGE OF DESIGNS.

Figure 10. Much jewellery makes use of patterned wires.

metal which are related to repoussé and stamping. For instance, a steel punch with a design engraved as an intaglio on the tip can be used to stamp a repeated pattern on to the metal, or a wooden punch can be used to drive a thin sheet of gold down into a die formed out of bronze or brass. Stamping, therefore, is not necessarily the mass-production technique which the name suggests.

Engraving

Engraving is perhaps the most widely used method of applying decoration to a metal surface (see figure 27). Although the tech-

Plate 6. An Indian bracelet, in silver, with eleven hinged units. The hollow 'ribbed' components are made from two pressings soldered together. Figure 9 illustrates the type of punch that was probably used.

Plate 7. Detail of the Indian bracelet showing the line of the solder joint on one of the units. Each of the flower motifs has a common fault on the design, indicating that they were stamped out using the same punch.

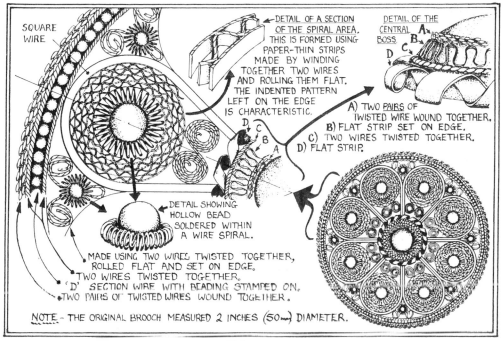

Figure 11. A filigree brooch analysed. This example, in silver, was made in Palestine in the 1940s.

nique is of ancient origin, it is dependent on the technology to manufacture iron of a hardness suitable for the engraving tools. These are called gravers. They are a form of short chisel fitted to a small rounded handle which nestles in the palm of the hand. Held at a shallow angle to the surface of the metal, the graver is pushed forward so that it excavates a tiny groove. Each cut of the graving tool is like a stroke of the calligrapher's pen: done well it can have a satisfying rightness about it. Also, like the mark of the pen, it is indelible.

Engine turning

The most familiar example of engine turning is the ornamental patterns which may be found engraved on the backs of gold or silver pocket watches. These fascinating geometric designs were carried out using an elaborate form of lathe called a rose engine. Other examples of machine engraving may be identified readily, even without an eyeglass, by the mechanical accuracy of every line.

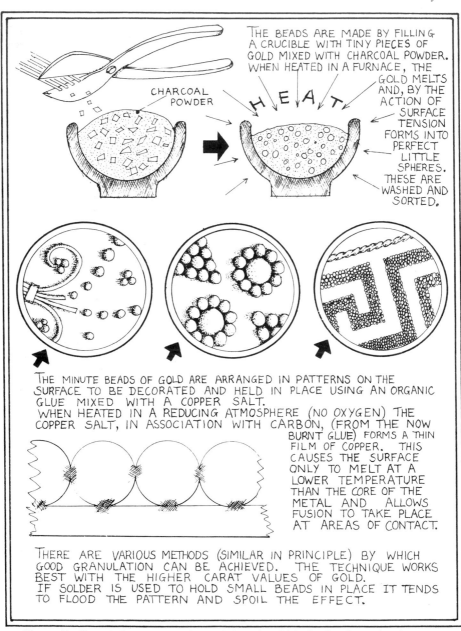

THE BEADS ARE MADE BY FILLING A CRUCIBLE WITH TINY PIECES OF GOLD MIXED WITH CHARCOAL POWDER. WHEN HEATED IN A FURNACE, THE GOLD MELTS AND, BY THE ACTION OF SURFACE TENSION FORMS INTO PERFECT LITTLE SPHERES. THESE ARE WASHED AND SORTED.

CHARCOAL POWDER

HEAT

THE MINUTE BEADS OF GOLD ARE ARRANGED IN PATTERNS ON THE SURFACE TO BE DECORATED AND HELD IN PLACE USING AN ORGANIC GLUE MIXED WITH A COPPER SALT.
WHEN HEATED IN A REDUCING ATMOSPHERE (NO OXYGEN) THE COPPER SALT, IN ASSOCIATION WITH CARBON, (FROM THE NOW BURNT GLUE) FORMS A THIN FILM OF COPPER. THIS CAUSES THE SURFACE ONLY TO MELT AT A LOWER TEMPERATURE THAN THE CORE OF THE METAL AND ALLOWS FUSION TO TAKE PLACE AT AREAS OF CONTACT.

THERE ARE VARIOUS METHODS (SIMILAR IN PRINCIPLE) BY WHICH GOOD GRANULATION CAN BE ACHIEVED. THE TECHNIQUE WORKS BEST WITH THE HIGHER CARAT VALUES OF GOLD.
IF SOLDER IS USED TO HOLD SMALL BEADS IN PLACE IT TENDS TO FLOOD THE PATTERN AND SPOIL THE EFFECT.

Figure 12. Granulation, a decorative technique in which tiny beads are fused on to a surface without the use of solder.

Filigree

This delicate method of making jewellery demands patience and skill from the craftsman. It depends upon an ample supply of very fine wire which is doubled over, twisted together and then rolled flat. This is the basic component of filigree and it is used on edge, scrolled and curved into delicate patterns which are fixed within an outer framework. Finely coiled wire, hollow beads and hemispheres are also used. The best filigree is open-backed (figure 11 shows details).

This is a highly vulnerable type of decoration, particularly if it is badly made. In cheaper work an especially low-temperature solder is often used, frequently to excess, so that the details of the pattern become flooded and clogged. Also, as a substitute for the flattened twisted wire, a plain flat strip with a serrated edge may often be found. Careful use of solder and an even application of heat are both critical factors in this type of work.

Granulation

Examples of granulation may be found in many pieces of old jewellery but none have equalled the quality of Etruscan work from the sixth century BC, when the craft was brought to a peak of perfection. The technique involves arranging into patterns countless minute beads or grains of gold and fusing them to the surface of the jewel (figure 12). Solder cannot be used because it floods the grains and ruins the effect, so a form of fusion soldering is essential. The exact way in which the Etruscans made their remarkable jewellery has been the subject of much speculation and experiment.

Metal inlay

Decoration using a different-coloured metal, for example gold on silver, or red, white and green gold on a yellow gold surface, is normally carried out by soldering the added pieces into place. This means that they are then proud of the surface. In order to set the decoration flush with the surface it can be inlaid by first recessing the design (by engraving or chiselling it out), then hammering in a contrasting metal, preferably soft, to fill the cavity. It is essential to key the bottom and sides of the recess in order to grip the decoration.

Cut steel

Jewellery made using cut steel was produced at Woodstock, among other places, and later at Birmingham both before and

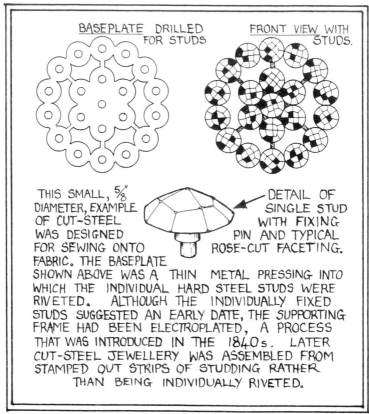

BASEPLATE DRILLED
FOR STUDS

FRONT VIEW WITH
STUDS.

THIS SMALL, ⅝″
DIAMETER, EXAMPLE
OF CUT-STEEL
WAS DESIGNED
FOR SEWING ONTO
FABRIC. THE BASEPLATE

DETAIL OF
SINGLE STUD
WITH FIXING
PIN AND TYPICAL
ROSE-CUT FACETING.

SHOWN ABOVE WAS A THIN METAL PRESSING INTO
WHICH THE INDIVIDUAL HARD STEEL STUDS WERE
RIVETED. ALTHOUGH THE INDIVIDUALLY FIXED
STUDS SUGGESTED AN EARLY DATE, THE SUPPORTING
FRAME HAD BEEN ELECTROPLATED, A PROCESS
THAT WAS INTRODUCED IN THE 1840s. LATER
CUT-STEEL JEWELLERY WAS ASSEMBLED FROM
STAMPED OUT STRIPS OF STUDDING RATHER
THAN BEING INDIVIDUALLY RIVETED.

Figure 13. Cut-steel jewellery.

after 1800. It is a distinctive type of work in which small faceted
steel rivets were arranged in tight patterns and fixed to a
backplate, often of brass (figure 13). Used for buckles and a wide
range of jewellery, the effect is reminiscent of the rose-cut diamonds which were then in use. *Marcasite* (faceted iron pyrites),
which came into use in Europe during the eighteenth century,
was similar in appearance to cut steel.

Even *cast iron* was used to make jewellery during the wars
between Prussia and France in the years following 1800.
Wonderfully intricate, it was made in Berlin and given to those
who did their patriotic duty by selling valuable jewels to pay for
the fighting.

The next types of decoration to be described are those which
involve the fixing of some different substance to the surface of

the metal. Principal amongst these are the gemstones but this wide subject is dealt with separately in chapters 7 to 10.

Enamel

As a way of bringing colour into a jewel without the use of gemstones, enamel has no equal. It can be used as a decorative adjunct simply by *encrusting* an area of gold, or it may, in the form of a painted miniature portrait, constitute the centrepiece of the jewel itself. Indeed, many finely done enamels are deservedly treated much as gemstones and set into a jewel with similar care.

Enamel is a transparent vitreous compound which is coloured by the addition of metal oxides. Ground up to form a coarse powder, it is packed on to the surface of the metal and heated until it melts into place. Although it will maintain a tenacious grip upon

Plate 8. An Edwardian ring in 18 carat gold (maker's initials EAM, Birmingham, 1908), with a peridot and two pink tourmalines, set in collets with millegrained edges. Both the design and the choice of stones are typical of the period.

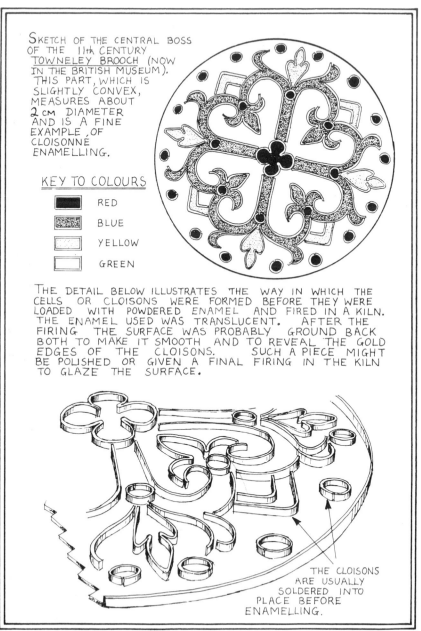

SKETCH OF THE CENTRAL BOSS
OF THE 11th CENTURY
TOWNELEY BROOCH (NOW
IN THE BRITISH MUSEUM).
THIS PART, WHICH IS
SLIGHTLY CONVEX,
MEASURES ABOUT
2 CM DIAMETER
AND IS A FINE
EXAMPLE , OF
CLOISONNÉ
ENAMELLING.

KEY TO COLOURS

██	RED
▒▒	BLUE
☐	YELLOW
☐	GREEN

THE DETAIL BELOW ILLUSTRATES THE WAY IN WHICH THE
CELLS OR CLOISONS WERE FORMED BEFORE THEY WERE
LOADED WITH POWDERED ENAMEL AND FIRED IN A KILN.
THE ENAMEL USED WAS TRANSLUCENT. AFTER THE
FIRING THE SURFACE WAS PROBABLY GROUND BACK
BOTH TO MAKE IT SMOOTH AND TO REVEAL THE GOLD
EDGES OF THE CLOISONS. SUCH A PIECE MIGHT
BE POLISHED OR GIVEN A FINAL FIRING IN THE KILN
TO GLAZE THE SURFACE.

THE CLOISONS
ARE USUALLY
SOLDERED INTO
PLACE BEFORE
ENAMELLING.

Figure 14. Cloisonné enamelling, in which the design is delineated by a thin metal strip
which forms cells to contain and separate the enamel.

the metal, it is a form of glass and so is liable to crack and flake off if it is not correctly applied. Usually a flat area of enamelling will also have been enamelled on the back (*counter-enamelled*) in order to balance the expansion and contraction forces which are set up in the metal.

There are a number of clearly identifiable ways in which enamel is used. *Cloisonné* is one of the more familiar methods, in which the lines of the design are marked out by thin gold fences to form a series of separate cells into which the enamel is laid and fired into place (figure 14). The surface may be ground back so that it is flat, and then polished, or it may be re-fired to give it a glazed finish.

Cells into which enamel can be packed may also be made by excavating them with an engraving tool or a small chisel. This is called *champlevé* where the finished surface of the enamel is level with the surrounding metal (figure 15).

If, however, the excavated area of metal is decorated with a pattern or a slightly raised design (bas-relief) and covered with a coloured but transparent enamel so that the decoration can be seen through it, the result is called *basse-taille*.

One of the more difficult, and relatively rare, techniques is *plique à jour,* whereby gold cells are filled with transparent enamel and left open at the base to give a stained-glass effect There are a number of ingenious ways of achieving this sensational but fragile result.

Painted enamels, also known as *Limoges,* require a great deal of artistic skill. The enamels themselves are ground to a very fine powder which allows a brush to be used to paint them on and there may be many stages of firing. *Grisaille* is a two-tone enamel painting technique in which the design is carried out in white enamel on a black or blue base colour.

There are other obscure enamelling methods but the principal ones have been mentioned.

Niello

This curious substance is a grey-black alloy of silver, copper and lead to which an excess of sulphur has been added. The resulting compound is ground up, packed into cells, recessed areas or engraved lines, then melted into place at low temperature. The surface may be polished or burnished and takes on a metallic lustre similar to that of haematite. This technique has ancient origins and is a surprisingly permanent form of decoration.

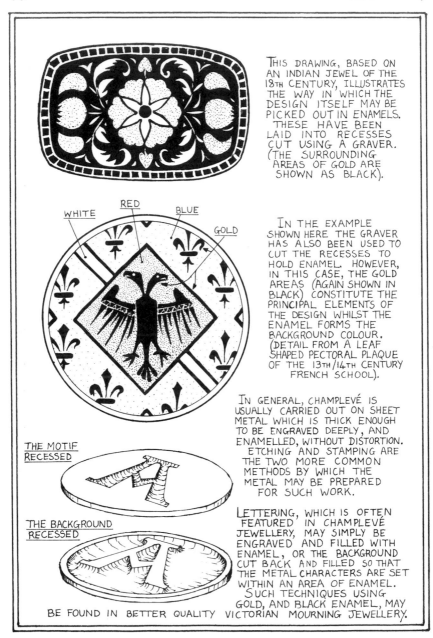

THIS DRAWING, BASED ON AN INDIAN JEWEL OF THE 18TH CENTURY, ILLUSTRATES THE WAY IN WHICH THE DESIGN ITSELF MAY BE PICKED OUT IN ENAMELS. THESE HAVE BEEN LAID INTO RECESSES CUT USING A GRAVER. (THE SURROUNDING AREAS OF GOLD ARE SHOWN AS BLACK).

WHITE   RED   BLUE   GOLD

IN THE EXAMPLE SHOWN HERE THE GRAVER HAS ALSO BEEN USED TO CUT THE RECESSES TO HOLD ENAMEL. HOWEVER, IN THIS CASE, THE GOLD AREAS (AGAIN SHOWN IN BLACK) CONSTITUTE THE PRINCIPAL ELEMENTS OF THE DESIGN WHILST THE ENAMEL FORMS THE BACKGROUND COLOUR. (DETAIL FROM A LEAF SHAPED PECTORAL PLAQUE OF THE 13TH/14TH CENTURY FRENCH SCHOOL).

IN GENERAL, CHAMPLEVÉ IS USUALLY CARRIED OUT ON SHEET METAL WHICH IS THICK ENOUGH TO BE ENGRAVED DEEPLY, AND ENAMELLED, WITHOUT DISTORTION. ETCHING AND STAMPING ARE THE TWO MORE COMMON METHODS BY WHICH THE METAL MAY BE PREPARED FOR SUCH WORK.

THE MOTIF RECESSED

THE BACKGROUND RECESSED

LETTERING, WHICH IS OFTEN FEATURED IN CHAMPLEVÉ JEWELLERY, MAY SIMPLY BE ENGRAVED AND FILLED WITH ENAMEL, OR THE BACKGROUND CUT BACK AND FILLED SO THAT THE METAL CHARACTERS ARE SET WITHIN AN AREA OF ENAMEL. SUCH TECHNIQUES USING GOLD, AND BLACK ENAMEL, MAY BE FOUND IN BETTER QUALITY VICTORIAN MOURNING JEWELLERY.

Figure 15. Champlevé enamelling.

Piqué work

Piqué is a decorative method in which tortoiseshell (usually) or horn is inlaid with silver, gold or mother-of-pearl (figure 16). *Piqué point,* which is composed of tiny wires pushed into the horn and then filed flush with the surface to leave a series of dots, is perhaps the most common form. Sometimes tiny star shapes are also used. In *piqué posé,* strips or larger areas of metal are pressed into the surface. A combination of piqué point and piqué posé is often found on the same piece of jewellery. The manufacture of piqué dates from before 1700 to about 1885.

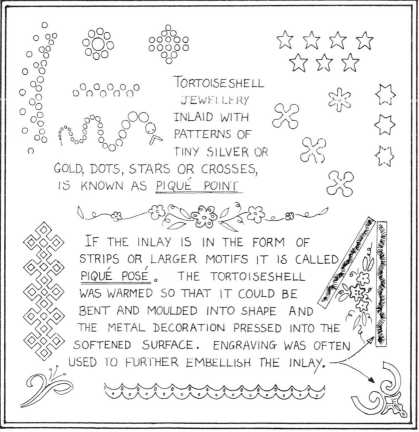

Figure 16. Piqué jewellery. These are typical pattern motifs. Later work often contains elaborate floral inlays.

Mosaic work

The creation of miniature landscape pictures using mosaics was carried out in Italy from the early nineteenth century. The most detailed form was *micro-mosaics* from Rome, in which the picture was built up using tiny tesserae, usually of coloured glass, which were cemented into place.

A second type of mosaic, different in character, came from Florence. This was built up from larger, carefully cut pieces of semi-precious stone (malachite, agate, cornelian, for example) set into a black background. These often used floral motifs and are known as *pietra dura*.

Inlay

Many of the above mentioned techniques are forms of inlay. Jewellery often involves the general use of inlay: the cementing of ivory, for example, into a recess in gold, or the fixing of accurately cut opaque glass into shaped cells.

Much jewellery is made with a combination of different techniques so that one is often forced to describe it as a 'sort of inlay' or a 'form of granulation'.

Plate 9. This 9 carat ring carried a Chester hallmark for 1884. The stones, which appeared to be original, were blue and white paste in imitation of sapphire and diamond. The settings and the ring itself were all of lightweight construction. Had the stones been real, the ring would probably have been a more robust structure and made in 18 carat gold.

3
The precious metals

This chapter deals with the metals gold, silver and platinum. Rolled gold is discussed in chapter 4.

Gold

If one were given the freedom to devise the perfect metal for making jewellery, there would be no need to improve upon gold: in addition to its spectacular colour, it is highly resistant to corrosion and both malleable and ductile to a degree that is unique in the family of metallic elements. It is a lustrous yellow metal of unparalleled beauty, with physical properties which make it ideal for the creation of fine jewellery.

Because gold is very valuable, the huge accumulated reserves of this superlative metal are locked away in bank vaults throughout the world and only a tiny proportion is destined ever to be used for ornament.

In its pure form gold is very soft and amazingly heavy, having something of the consistency of lead but approaching twice the weight. (Figure 19 shows the relative weights of the precious metals.) Its ductility allows it to be drawn through dies to make a very thin wire, while most metals will tear apart if this is tried, and it can be beaten out to make sheets which are so extremely thin that light can pass through them.

The softness of pure gold is, however, a disadvantage for most applications, so the working properties are modified by the addition of other metals to form an alloy. All golds used for making jewellery are alloys of some sort. The proportion by weight of this added metal is indicated by the *carat* value (figure 17). Pure gold, for example, is 24 carat, that is 24 parts of gold in every 24. (In practice, for normal purposes, pure or fine gold is made to a purity of 99.9 per cent.) Thus 18 carat gold is 18/24ths, which is a purity of 75 per cent, and 9 carat is half that, at 37.5 per cent, which is the lowest legal gold standard for British jewellery.

This alloying or dilution of the gold does not seriously impair its corrosion resistance and it has the following benefits:

1. The *working properties* of the gold can be modified to suit it to any particular application. For example, an alloy used for casting would need to have good molten flow characteristics whilst gold which is to be rolled into a thin sheet might well need good cold

Figure 17. The carat values of gold. These are indications of the ratio of gold to other metal by weight. The illustrations here are for red alloys of gold (using copper) whereas in practice many different mixtures of metal can be added to the gold to alter its properties.

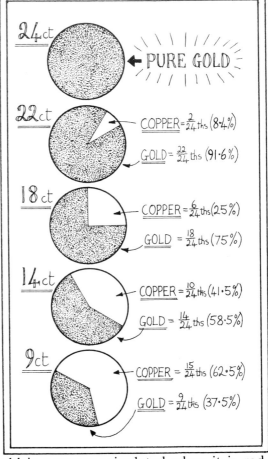

flow characteristics. Gold is never manipulated when it is red-hot, because at high temperatures, before melting, it assumes the consistency of crumbling cheese. So, unlike steel, it is always worked cold. However, the metal will work-harden and crack if it is not periodically heated and quenched (annealed) to relieve the stresses.

2. The *colour* of the alloy can be altered within certain limits by the addition of other metals, the most striking change being achieved by using nickel, zinc or palladium to make a white gold. The yellow of the gold will, however, often show through slightly, so it has for some years been common practice to

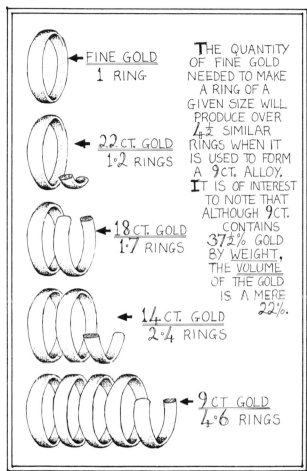

FINE GOLD
1 RING

22 CT. GOLD
1·2 RINGS

18 CT. GOLD
1·7 RINGS

14 CT. GOLD
2·4 RINGS

9 CT GOLD
4·6 RINGS

THE QUANTITY OF FINE GOLD NEEDED TO MAKE A RING OF A GIVEN SIZE WILL PRODUCE OVER $4\frac{1}{2}$ SIMILAR RINGS WHEN IT IS USED TO FORM A 9 CT. ALLOY. IT IS OF INTEREST TO NOTE THAT ALTHOUGH 9 CT. CONTAINS $37\frac{1}{2}$% GOLD BY WEIGHT, THE VOLUME OF THE GOLD IS A MERE 22%.

Figure 18. An illustration of the way in which the 'dilution' of pure gold to form the lower carat values is highly advantageous in terms of the increase in volume.

electro-plate the surface with rhodium.

Other colours are more subtle: thus a red or pink gold is the result of adding copper; silver will give a greenish tinge, whilst the presence of iron can add a hint of blue. Because 22 carat gold contains a mere 8.4 per cent of other metal there is very little scope for modifying the colour of this particular alloy.

Many Victorian brooches feature a wide variety of different shades of gold. Frequently the colours show up better if the metal has lost its bright polish.

3. The *melting point* of an alloy may be changed by the selective addition of even small quantities of particular metals. Thus by

adding zinc (melting point 418°C) a series of different solders may be made. For 9 carat gold these could range from an 'extra easy' one at 650°C up to a 'hard' solder at 780°C, whilst the alloy itself might melt at 900°C.

4. The *cost*. By the simple expedient of making an alloy more pieces of jewellery may be produced from a given amount of pure gold. For example, if a fine gold ring of a particular fixed size was melted down and mixed with enough copper to create a 9 carat alloy it would be possible to make four and a half identical rings from the resulting metal (see figure 18).

Many pieces of old gold jewellery retain a bright finish in spite of their age and the fact that they may have been made from a low-carat alloy. The colour of the surface often resembles that of pure gold, which may suggest that the work has been gilded. Although this is sometimes so, the richness of the yellow may be the result of one of the *surface enrichment* techniques which were used during the nineteenth century for improving the appearance of the work. This involved dissolving out the copper just at the surface of the alloy so that a very thin layer of fine gold remained as a rich coating to impress the customer. An attractive feature of this method of finishing was the matt, rather than shiny surface, which was caused by the etching effect of the acid used. One of the surface enrichment methods used was known as *wet colouring;* it was a somewhat hazardous process as is indicated by the following contemporary account:
'Gold-workers are exposed to several pernicious vapours in the exercise of their trade, by far the worst being that which arises during the process of wet-colouring, from the action of the spirits of salts upon the work and the other ingredients. The effluvia arising therefrom, in badly constructed workrooms, produces great distress to the operator, affecting the head, the stomach, and the whole nervous system. When the above symptoms present themselves, a good drink of new milk will counteract the evil, and act as a complete antidote to the mischievous effects of the poisonous and other noxious vapours, taken into the stomach during the performance of any of these processes.'

Silver
Silver is a white metal which, like gold, is too soft for making jewellery in its pure form, although it is sometimes used to make

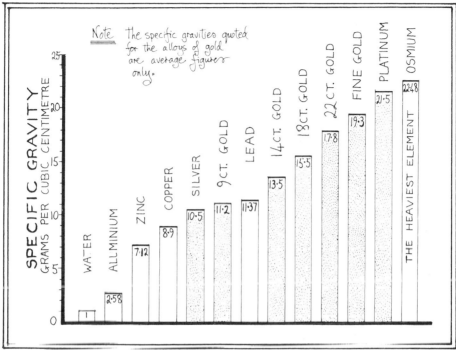

Figure 19. Diagram showing the approximate relative weights or densities of the precious metals. With experience it is possible to estimate the carat value of gold simply by its weight in the hand. It will be noted that fine gold is nearly twice the weight of lead.

the bezel and other settings for delicate gemstones. Because it is soft it is mixed with a small amount of copper to create an alloy which in Great Britain is known as *standard silver* or more usually *sterling silver*. This alloy, which is 92.5 per cent silver, is also referred to as 925 (parts per thousand) silver.

Although silver is slightly less resistant to corrosion than gold and does tend to tarnish, it is a very good metal for the manufacture of jewellery because it has excellent working properties and is capable of being given a superb polished finish.

With a specific gravity of 10.5, fine silver is about half the weight of fine gold (specific gravity 19.3) but only slightly lighter than 9 carat gold (specific gravity about 11.2). (Specific gravity, or density, is the weight of the metal in relation to the weight of an identical volume of water. Thus fine gold is 19.3 times heavier than water. See figure 19.)

Silver solders of a 92.5 per cent standard are made by replacing a small proportion of the 7.5 per cent copper with a metal such as zinc, which, with its low melting point, lowers the melting point of the alloy. A typical series of solders for use with sterling silver (melting point approximately 850°C) covers the temperature range from 675°C for 'extra easy' solder to a 'hard ' solder of 780°C.

A silver solder joint, however well made, can always be found if the metal is heated slightly because the alloy in the joint oxidises at a different rate from the parent metal. Such detective work is vital in the repair of old jewellery.

Silver alloys do have a disadvantage because at red heat (when soldering or annealing) the copper content forms a very thin but hard layer of copper oxide within the surface of the metal. Known as *fire stain,* this has the effect of clouding a brightly polished surface. The stain can be removed by filing, but only with difficulty, so frequently it is disguised by giving the work a thin plating of fine silver. Alternatively, as with much jewellery, it can be ignored and the surface given a less bright polish so that the fire stain is no longer apparent. Gold alloys do not suffer from this problem.

Platinum

Platinum is a heavy, soft and ductile metal, grey-white in colour and with excellent corrosion resistance. It is one of the most permanent of metals. Its specific gravity of 21.45 makes it slightly heavier even than pure gold and about twice the weight of silver.

One of its most unusual properties is the melting point of 1773°C, which is very high when compared with gold, at 1062°C, and silver at only 960°C. Jewellery manufacturers and craftsmen of the nineteenth century and earlier would have experienced considerable difficulty in achieving temperatures in excess of 1500°C and this is one of the reasons why the wider use of platinum for jewellery dates only from about 1920.

It has been found that the addition of just 5 per cent of other metal is enough to allow the working properties to be suitably modified for jewellery and a purity of 95 per cent (known as the 950 standard) is widely accepted. (The hallmarking of platinum did not begin in Great Britain until 1975.)

Apart from providing the material to make complete jewels, it has long been used for the settings on gold rings because claws of platinum can be pushed over to hold a gemstone very firmly without having any tendency to spring back.

4
Rolled gold, base metals and plating

Jewellery made in base metal is usually an attempt to imitate a precious metal, so that yellow brass and bronze are got up to look like gold and nickel alloys seek to pass as silver. Few people are taken in by this unless the piece is plated with gold or silver, when one is compelled to search in vain for hallmarks or to scrape and test the metal. However, old jewellery does not have to be made from valuable materials in order to be interesting.

Brass

Copper is a soft red metal which has rather poor working properties until it is combined with another metal. Thus with just a small addition of zinc it is possible to create the immensely useful alloy known as brass, which is harder and stronger than either of its constituents. The exact quantity of zinc which needs to be added to copper varies according to the use. *Gilding metal,* for instance, is a form of brass which may contain 95 per cent copper and only 5 per cent zinc. It is, as its name suggests, used for making jewellery which is subsequently to be gold-plated. The proportion of zinc in brass can be higher than 50 per cent, and other metals, such as tin, nickel and lead, are often added to modify the properties. The melting points for the different brasses range from 900°C to 1050°C and are similar to those for the alloys of gold.

Pinchbeck

Brass that includes from 12 to 15 per cent zinc is very similar in colour to gold. This fact was noted by a London watchmaker by the name of Christopher Pinchbeck (1670-1732), who promoted its use for cheap jewellery. Thus 'pinchbeck' became the term used for a brass alloy which imitated gold. It is possible that there was also some secret process for applying a thin wash of gold to the surface, but the metal probably found particular favour at that time because the official hallmark standards for gold were high (18 and 22 carats), thus putting precious metal jewellery out of reach of the common man. With the introduction of 9, 12 and 15 carat standards in 1854 and with the then new process of electro-gilding, the use of pinchbeck dwindled.

Bronze

Bronze is an alloy of copper and tin and a number of grades have been in use for making jewellery. A 10 to 15 per cent tin content is common, giving a pale red colour which can be chemically coloured to enrich the surface. This copper-rich alloy has been widely used for enamelled items. The use of bronze in ancient jewellery predates brass because in the past zinc was much more difficult to obtain than tin.

Often it is difficult to be precise about whether a copper-based alloy is brass or bronze since compositions are used which contain both zinc and tin.

Nickel silver

Nickel silver is a white alloy based on a mixture of copper (65 per cent), nickel (18 per cent) and zinc (17 per cent). It does not contain silver but rather resembles it. A very similar alloy is known as *German silver.*

Rolled gold

The production of rolled gold took place in Birmingham following the invention of the process in 1785 by a London manufacturer. It is a particularly durable form of gold plating which is carried out by soldering a thick sheet of say 9 or 18 carat gold to an even thicker sheet of brass, in the ratio of perhaps 1:20. This double layer is then rolled down to form a thin sheet which is used to make the jewellery (figure 20). During the rolling process the 1:20 ratio of the two layers remains constant and, although the gold alloy on the surface may end up only a few thousandths of an inch thick, because it is a tough alloy of gold it will be hardwearing. Rolled gold is also made in the form of solid and hollow wire, both of which have been used widely for chainmaking.

Before the introduction of electro-gilding during the 1840s, rolled gold was known as gold plating.

In the 1870s in the United States a double form of rolled gold, which had been introduced for making pocket-watch cases, was given the name *gold-filled.* This was simply a base metal with a gold alloy soldered on both sides.

Rolled gold was a natural development of the concept behind *Sheffield plate,* which had been invented by Thomas Bolsover in 1742. This consisted of a thin layer of silver on a base of copper and remained in use for over a century until electro-plating was invented, simplifying the business of making cheap flatware.

Its relatively light weight allows at least a preliminary identifi-

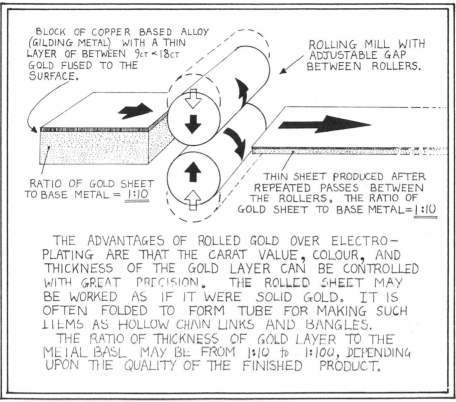

THE ADVANTAGES OF ROLLED GOLD OVER ELECTRO-
PLATING ARE THAT THE CARAT VALUE, COLOUR, AND
THICKNESS OF THE GOLD LAYER CAN BE CONTROLLED
WITH GREAT PRECISION. THE ROLLED SHEET MAY
BE WORKED AS IF IT WERE SOLID GOLD. IT IS
OFTEN FOLDED TO FORM TUBE FOR MAKING SUCH
ITEMS AS HOLLOW CHAIN LINKS AND BANGLES.
THE RATIO OF THICKNESS OF GOLD LAYER TO THE
METAL BASE MAY BE FROM 1:10 to 1:100, DEPENDING
UPON THE QUALITY OF THE FINISHED PRODUCT.

Figure 20. Rolled gold, which may take the form of wire, sheet or tube, is made by fusing a layer of gold alloy to a thick base of copper alloy (usually), then rolling or drawing it down to the final dimensions.

cation of rolled gold. The base alloy of brass, with a specific gravity of 8.5, is noticeably lighter than 9 carat gold (specific gravity about 11.2) and with experience the difference is surprisingly easy to discern.

An example of a brooch made in rolled gold is shown in figure 21.

Fire gilding

The earliest technique for applying a layer of gold to a base-metal surface was fire gilding, a potentially lethal process which exposed the luckless worker to mercury oxide vapours. The procedure was to mix mercury and pure gold together to form an amalgam which was spread evenly over the surface of the work to

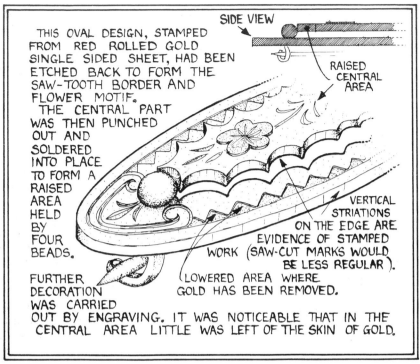

SIDE VIEW

THIS OVAL DESIGN, STAMPED
FROM RED ROLLED GOLD
SINGLE SIDED SHEET, HAD BEEN
ETCHED BACK TO FORM THE
SAW-TOOTH BORDER AND
FLOWER MOTIF.
    THE CENTRAL PART
WAS THEN PUNCHED
OUT AND
SOLDERED
INTO PLACE
TO FORM A
RAISED
AREA
HELD
BY
FOUR
BEADS.

RAISED
CENTRAL
AREA

VERTICAL
STRIATIONS
ON THE EDGE ARE
EVIDENCE OF STAMPED
WORK (SAW-CUT MARKS WOULD
BE LESS REGULAR).

FURTHER
DECORATION
WAS CARRIED

(LOWERED AREA WHERE
GOLD HAS BEEN REMOVED.

OUT BY ENGRAVING. IT WAS NOTICEABLE THAT IN THE
CENTRAL AREA LITTLE WAS LEFT OF THE SKIN OF GOLD.

Figure 21. A late nineteenth-century rolled-gold brooch. Detail of one end only.

be plated. It was then heated to drive off the mercury, leaving
behind a layer of pure gold. It was also known as *mercury
gilding*. The decline of this hazardous trade began with the introduction of electro-gilding in the 1840s.

Electro-plating

This process of depositing either silver or gold on to a base
metal by the use of an electric current was developed in the years
after 1840 in Birmingham by G. R. and H. Elkington. The invention, by Dr Wright of Sheffield, was of immense importance for it
helped sustain the leading position which Birmingham held in the
mass-production of jewellery and small work. As already mentioned, electro-plating spelled the end of mercury gilding and the
demise of the Sheffield plate industry.

Pewter

There is a variety of alloys whose principal component is tin:

all of them are forms of pewter. They may or may not also contain lead, bismuth, copper or antimony. In general a pewter alloy is softer than silver yet harder than lead; it has a low melting point, of about 300°C, so may be cast into rubber moulds for making inexpensive costume jewellery. Such castings are often heavily plated to give the pewter a harder and more durable surface and to reinforce the structure.

White metal and *Britannia metal* (not to be confused with Britannia silver) are both widely used forms of pewter.

Iron and steel

The ferrous metals are seldom used for jewellery because they are tough to work, melt only at high temperatures and have a tendency to rust. In spite of this there have been periods when *cast iron* jewellery has been made and this is now much sought after by collectors. The pieces, made in Germany and France, show an astonishing delicacy of detail and are fine examples of the founder's art. Cast iron is very brittle, which makes its use for jewellery rather surprising.

Cut steel jewellery and decorative accessories were made during the eighteenth and early nineteenth centuries. (A small example is shown in figure 13.) These used elaborate arrangements of cut and faceted studs, which, because they were of a hard polished steel, did have some resistance to rust.

Plate 10. A very finely engraved silver brooch of hollow construction, dating from the late nineteenth century; diameter 51 mm (2 inches).

5
The workshop of the goldsmith and jeweller

The romantic notion of a supremely skilled goldsmith working at his bench making elaborate masterpieces, in dedicated isolation, is far from reality. The manufacture of jewellery, even of very valuable pieces, is almost invariably the joint labour of many specialist craftsmen. This specialisation is essential where work of the highest quality is being made. For example, the art of enamelling demands an intimate knowledge of the melting range of many different enamels and the necessary skill must be exercised constantly in order to be able to judge correctly the timing and temperature. Likewise, the stone setter must use his considerable skills regularly in order to cope efficiently with this very difficult and concentrated work.

Thus the goldsmith who attempts to embrace all the skills of his craft is likely to be slow and inefficient, liable to make mistakes and, above all, unable to produce high-quality work in every department.

A modern craftsman suddenly transported to a mid nineteenth-century workshop would find himself so familiar with almost every piece of equipment that he would be able to sit at the bench and immediately begin working gold.

In the nineteenth century, as in every jewellery workshop of the past, the craftsmen would have been seated at the *jeweller's board* or workbench, made using a thick slab of wood from which a series of semicircles had been cut (figure 22). Groups of three or five men to a bench were a common arrangement, each man seated on a three-legged stool, the top of which was sometimes made from the offcut wood. The cut-out in the bench gave the craftsman a good working position with an area on each side to steady and rest his arms. Slung across within the semicircle was the leather *skin,* arranged to catch the steady rain of filings and offcuts of gold and silver. The seating was usually low and the bench set at a height so that its surface was near to eye level. Fixed centrally in the curved edge of the bench was the wedge-shaped hardwood *bench peg* or pin, which provided essential support for the workpiece, while to one side, almost at the jeweller's elbow, was a horizontal gas jet which emitted a flickering yellow flame. He used this for heating the jewellery when solder-

Figure 22. A jewellery workshop of the late eighteenth century showing the bench with its semicircular workplaces grouped at a window. Within the cut-outs can be seen the bench peg or pin, which acted as a work rest, and below this the leather skin, which was intended to catch any scrap gold. The two glass globes on stands were filled with water and used to concentrate light on to the workpiece. The floor was covered with a wooden grid which, by retaining scrap metal within the openings, stopped the loss of gold from the workshop on the soles of the craftsmen's shoes. (From Diderot's *Encyclopedia*, c.1770.)

ing. The work, supported on a wire *wig*, would be held up to the flame, which was then intensified with the aid of a small blowpipe held in the mouth.

In the days before electricity the workbenches would have been arranged around the window in order to make the most of the daylight. Oil lamps and gas lighting would have been a usable alternative. An aid to lighting in the workshop was the *water lamp*, a glass globe filled with water, which was set on a stand and positioned so as to concentrate light upon the work.

One of the most interesting features of the workshop would have been the floor, which might well have been covered in sheet iron or zinc in order to prevent particles of gold from being lost

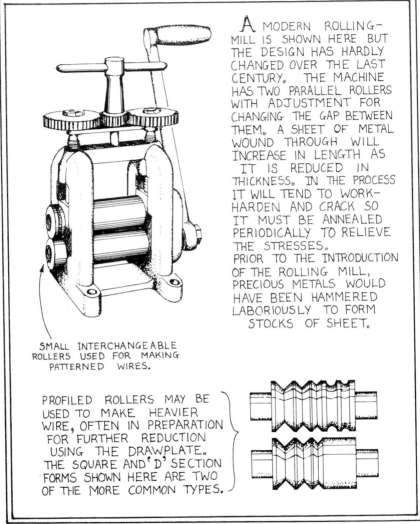

A MODERN ROLLING-MILL IS SHOWN HERE BUT THE DESIGN HAS HARDLY CHANGED OVER THE LAST CENTURY. THE MACHINE HAS TWO PARALLEL ROLLERS WITH ADJUSTMENT FOR CHANGING THE GAP BETWEEN THEM. A SHEET OF METAL WOUND THROUGH WILL INCREASE IN LENGTH AS IT IS REDUCED IN THICKNESS. IN THE PROCESS IT WILL TEND TO WORK-HARDEN AND CRACK SO IT MUST BE ANNEALED PERIODICALLY TO RELIEVE THE STRESSES.
PRIOR TO THE INTRODUCTION OF THE ROLLING MILL, PRECIOUS METALS WOULD HAVE BEEN HAMMERED LABORIOUSLY TO FORM STOCKS OF SHEET.

SMALL INTERCHANGEABLE ROLLERS USED FOR MAKING PATTERNED WIRES.

PROFILED ROLLERS MAY BE USED TO MAKE HEAVIER WIRE, OFTEN IN PREPARATION FOR FURTHER REDUCTION USING THE DRAWPLATE. THE SQUARE AND 'D' SECTION FORMS SHOWN HERE ARE TWO OF THE MORE COMMON TYPES.

Figure 23. The rolling mill.

through cracks in the floorboards. Over this metal surface would be laid a grating made of wood or iron, which served to scrape from the worker's shoes any grains of precious metal, causing them to fall and collect within the grid for later recovery.

Also to reduce the losses of gold within the workshop, it would have been a rule that the workers had to wash their hands at dinner time and at night using a special sink linked to a series of settling tanks for recovering the metal. Even the workers' aprons were washed on the premises and the gold was extracted from the waste water.

The craftsmen themselves were never entirely trusted because at the beginning of the day the gold would have been weighed out to each man, then when the work was finished the metal had to be checked back in, along with the day's *lemel* (offcuts and filings) and, with a tiny allowance of about 1 per cent for losses, the weights had to agree.

In addition to workbenches, the workshop would have contained at least two important mechanical devices, the *rolling mill* (figure 23) and the *drawbench,* both of which were vital aids to the speedy manipulation of metal. The rolling mill had a pair of cylindrical rollers with an adjustable gap and was used to make flat sheets. It might also have been fitted with grooved rollers,

Figure 24. The drawplate is used for making wire. A drawbench is needed when heavier gauges are drawn.

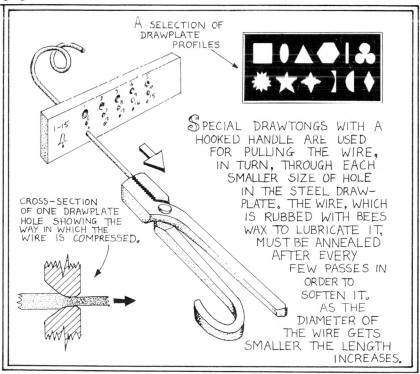

A SELECTION OF DRAWPLATE PROFILES

CROSS-SECTION OF ONE DRAWPLATE HOLE SHOWING THE WAY IN WHICH THE WIRE IS COMPRESSED.

SPECIAL DRAWTONGS WITH A HOOKED HANDLE ARE USED FOR PULLING THE WIRE, IN TURN, THROUGH EACH SMALLER SIZE OF HOLE IN THE STEEL DRAW-PLATE. THE WIRE, WHICH IS RUBBED WITH BEES WAX TO LUBRICATE IT, MUST BE ANNEALED AFTER EVERY FEW PASSES IN ORDER TO SOFTEN IT. AS THE DIAMETER OF THE WIRE GETS SMALLER THE LENGTH INCREASES.

containing various profiles, which could be used for forming rolled bars and wire. The drawbench was a form of winch which was used for pulling wire through a drawplate (figure 24) in order to reduce its diameter. Often the drawbench was a simple contraption, constructed from wood and using a heavy leather strap to connect the drawtongs to a type of capstan winch.

Variations on this form of workshop were used by a wide range of craftsmen associated with the jewellery trade. There was considerable subdivision within the industry, much of which was intended to facilitate the production of the goods in quantity.

For example, in the nineteenth century one would have found concentrated in the jewellery quarter of many cities a great diversity of craftsmen identified as stone cutters, setters, polishers, gilders, chasers, improvers, jobbers, pattern makers, chainmakers, enamellers, engravers and makers of wire and sheet. Sometimes the various crafts were concentrated beneath one roof but more often they were scattered throughout the quarter. Thus a single complex jewel or batch of jewellery might pass through a succession of workshops on its journey to completion.

Figure 25. Most jewellery workshops would be equipped to make gold or silver wire and sheet.

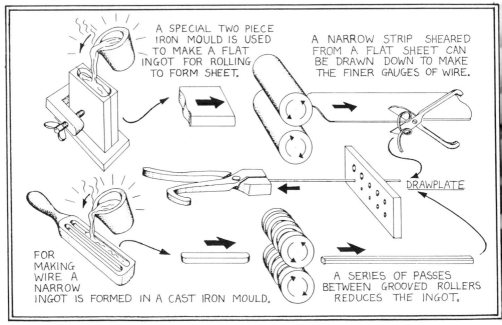

6
The craft of the goldsmith and jeweller

The skills of the goldsmith have changed little over the centuries. His craft was, and still is, one of delicate judgement and painstaking care. A good craftsman can seem almost like a magician in the way he manipulates the materials, always knowing exactly how to arrive, by the shortest possible route, at the splendour of the finished article. Jewellery of the finest quality has always been made by hand.

Most of the techniques used in making jewellery take advantage of the fact that the precious metals are remarkably malleable and ductile and can, with ease, be rolled or hammered to make flat sheet or rolled and drawn down to make wire. They are also easy to cut with the saw, the chisel or with shears and may readily be shaped with the file.

Typically a piece of jewellery will be made up from a number of individually shaped components which have been soldered together. The joints, if they are well done, will be at least unobtrusive, at best invisible.

Preparing the gold

So how did the goldsmith of, say, the eighteenth century start? He could not buy from the bullion dealer beautifully polished sheets of gold ready to use; he had to purchase fine gold by the troy ounce (31.1 grams) and from this prepare his own alloys and make such wire, sheet, tube and solders as the work demanded. After carefully weighing the ingredients he would drop them into a fireclay crucible, which was placed on the glowing coke or charcoal of a small furnace. A draught of air from large bellows would soon have raised the temperature and turned the gold into a molten pool of metal.

The next stage was to give it a preliminary shape by pouring it into an iron mould, which was designed to produce either a flat ingot, if sheet was required, or a long narrow ingot for the subsequent production of wire (figure 25). The mould was oiled before use, so the molten gold, when poured, generated clouds of smoke. The purpose of the iron was to chill the alloy as rapidly as possible in order to improve the condition of the metal.

The flat ingot was then repeatedly wound between the steel rollers of the rolling mill, with the gap being reduced at each pass of the metal. Since this caused the gold to work-harden and even crack, the metal would periodically be annealed by raising it to red heat and then quenching it (usually in acid, to remove any surface oxides). Rolling large pieces of gold sheet would have been work for strong men in the days before the widespread use of steam power and the electric motor.

Similar treatment in the rolling mill would have been given to the narrow ingot, passing it between the grooved rollers in order to reduce its diameter ready for the drawplate. Alternatively narrow strips could have been cut from the rolled sheet and drawn down to make wire.

Wire drawing

The *drawplate* in its simplicity is an elegant device. Iron versions were in use by AD 500, although drilled agate dies serving the same purpose may have been used as early as 2500 BC. The drawplate itself consists of an iron or steel bar through which a series of punched holes has been made. These cover various ranges in stepped sizes (see figure 24).

In order to make his wire, the craftsman would have tapered the end of the gold rod, pushed it into the first hole and hauled it through with drawtongs. As he worked down through the holes in this way, the wire would steadily have increased in length and, as with rolling sheet, it also would occasionally have needed annealing. A little beeswax rubbed on to the surface would have lubricated the operation.

Drawplates can be made with holes of various profiles, so it is easy to produce wire of any shape: oval, triangular, square and D-section for instance. A clear indication that a wire has been made using a drawplate is given by the minute striations which are left on the surface.

For making heavier gauges of wire it is necessary to use the drawbench, a winch arrangement attached to heavy tongs, designed to grip the wire tighter as the pull increases. For diameters below about 1.5 mm (0.060 inch) it is possible to pull the wire through with hand-held tongs. With long wires there is seldom room to pull the full length so the craftsman will turn on the spot and wind the wire around himself. Very long drawings need rotating drums to wind the wire through the plate.

The drill, the file and the saw

Once he had the correct metal stock to work from, the jeweller had simply to cut, shape and assemble the component parts for

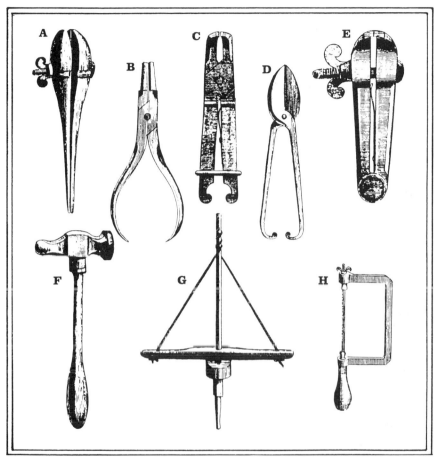

Figure 26. Illustrations from Diderot's *Encyclopedia* (c.1770) showing a selection of jeweller's tools, all of which are in production today: A, wooden clamp for holding rings; B, round-nosed pliers for bending wire; C, clamp with sliding locking ring; D, shears; E, hand-held vice; F, chasing hammer; G, jeweller's drill stock or bob drill; H, piercing saw.

the jewellery itself. For this task he had a number of basic tools, the most important of which were the drill, the file, the saw and the graver or burin.

The jeweller's *drill stock,* or *pump drill* (figure 26), with its miniature flywheel, possibly dates from 3000 BC, at which time it was used for lapidary work. Also known as a *bob drill,* it is still in use today. It has the important advantage of being usable when held in one hand only; this is vital because the workpiece had to

Plate 11. A bar brooch in a neat design from the 1930s. The aquamarine is held by a collet with millegrain edge. The main structure is formed in yellow gold but the entire front surface is covered with a thin layer of white gold.

be supported in the other. Starting with the cord wound up around the staff, a gentle downward pressure on the crossbar serves to spin the flywheel and turn the drill, the motion carrying through to rewind the cord in the opposite direction, back around the staff, at the same time lifting the bar up again, ready for the next power stroke. Since the direction of rotation was not constant, the drill could only be 50 per cent efficient because the cutting action was restricted to alternate strokes. The drill was used for such tasks as cutting seatings for stones intended for beaded settings (see figure 47) and for pierced work in combination with the saw.

The *file*, as it is manufactured today, with very fine precise cuts, is a sophisticated product but in the eighteenth century it must have been somewhat crude and therefore less useful for delicate work. Whilst a coarse file is good for removing metal, it leaves a scored surface which has then to be smoothed laboriously by hand, using abrasives.

The *jeweller's saw* (figure 26), in its modern form, is an elementary device but the blades are certainly not. Those made with the finest cut have as many as a hundred teeth to the inch (25 mm) and are manufactured to a very high standard. The eighteenth-century craftsman would not have had such a good product so it is likely that his saw was reserved for heavier work. However, in the hands of a skilled man it would still have been capable of producing an accurate finished edge needing little or no subsequent tidying.

Engraving

Used in jewellery far less now than in the past is the *engraving tool,* generally known as the *graver* or *burin* (figure 27). It is a small hand-held chisel, made in a variety of shapes with such names as *spitsticker, lozenge, onglette* and *knife.* Today it is mostly used by the engraver of lettering or patterns, but in older jewellery its use was more as a tool for removing metal — for shaping the form of the gold. It was like a sharp finger that could excavate holes or trenches in the jewellery and often it was the means of creating a deeply modelled piece of work, in effect carving the gold, a very satisfying skill when working in the higher carat values of gold.

In the eighteenth century the method often used for engraving a name or inscription was that of cutting away the background to leave raised lettering, the opposite of the intaglio technique which is common today (see the lower drawing in figure 15).

The graver is also a vital tool for the setting of stones and this is a particularly demanding aspect of the craft, requiring great patience and skill. (This subject is dealt with in chapter 10.)

Figure 27. The engraver's tools.

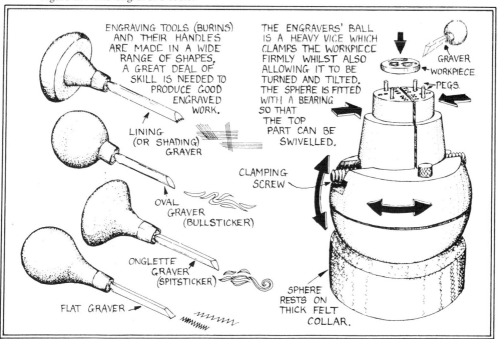

HERE THE HEAT SOURCE
IS AN OIL LAMP WITH A
WICK FITTED IN THE SPOUT.
  A HIGH TEMPERATURE IS
ACHIEVED BY USING A
BLOWPIPE TO FEED EXTRA
OXYGEN INTO THE FLAME.
  THE EXACT WAY IN
WHICH THE SMALL ITEM
BEING SOLDERED IS
HELD, IS NOT CLEAR
BUT IT MAY SIMPLY
BE CLAMPED IN A
HAND-HELD VICE OR
FIXED ON A BLOCK OF
CHARCOAL.
  IT WOULD HAVE BEEN
NECESSARY TO FLUX THE
WORK AND PLACE TINY
PIECES OF SOLDER IN
POSITION BEFORE APPLYING HEAT BECAUSE IT
WAS NOT POSSIBLE TO MANIPULATE THE JOB
DURING SOLDERING.
  IN THE 19TH CENTURY THE COAL GAS FLAME
GRADUALLY REPLACED THE OIL LAMP ALTHOUGH
THE BLOWPIPE REMAINED IN USE.

Figure 28. Soldering: an illustration from Diderot's *Encyclopedia* of c.1770.

Soldering

A fundamental feature of all jewellery is the *solder joint,* which is a means of permanently fixing together two pieces of metal by melting a lower-temperature alloy so that it flows into the gap between them. A piece of jewellery will usually be constructed to include the minimum number of solder joints.

Such a joint is made by binding the parts together using thin

Plate 12. This small silver brooch, its perimeter decorated with beads, is typical of work from the 1880s. The central raised motif has been stamped out and soldered into place. The engraving is somewhat crude, but effective.

Plate 13. Rear view of the silver brooch showing the hallmark of the Birmingham assay office for 1887 (maker's mark RJW).

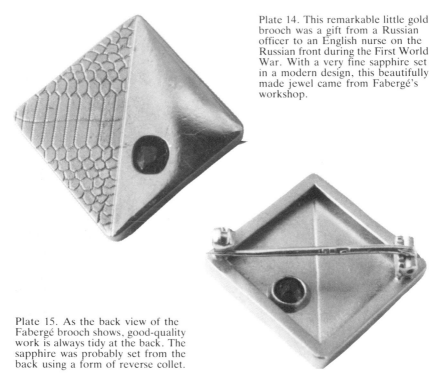

Plate 14. This remarkable little gold brooch was a gift from a Russian officer to an English nurse on the Russian front during the First World War. With a very fine sapphire set in a modern design, this beautifully made jewel came from Fabergé's workshop.

Plate 15. As the back view of the Fabergé brooch shows, good-quality work is always tidy at the back. The sapphire was probably set from the back using a form of reverse collet.

iron wire, then coating the contact area with a borax flux before laying tiny clippings of solder (paillons) in place. When heat is applied, the flux melts to form a glassy coating which keeps oxygen away (preventing the formation of oxides) and assists the smooth flow of the molten solder into the joint. The flux is subsequently removed with dilute sulphuric acid.

The solder used in precious jewellery is normally made to the same carat standard or quality as the main piece. The solder used by jewellers should not be confused with the structurally inferior soft solder, which is a lead-based alloy commonly used for making joints in plumbing and electrical work.

Soldering requires fine judgement and timing. The amount of solder used must fill the joint, not overflow it, and the temperature needs to be right.

In the eighteenth century the oil lamp and the blowpipe became available for soldering work (figure 28), although larger pieces would have been fluxed and wired up, with solder in place, before being heated in a small furnace. The famous Italian goldsmith Benvenuto Cellini, working in the sixteenth century, used such a technique, which he described in his *Treatise on Goldsmithing and Sculpture:* 'When you are ready to begin soldering, and want to make your solder flow, put your work in the furnace, and place beneath it a few little pieces of well dried wood, fanning them a bit with your bellows. Then it is not a bad thing, too, after this to throw a few coarse cinders upon the fire,

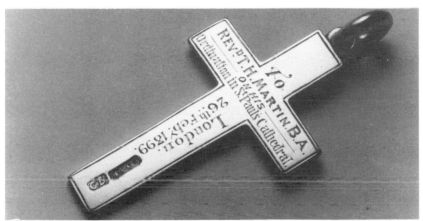

Plate 16. A substantial gold cross with a wonderfully informative inscription on the back. In addition, the maker's mark is CB followed by '15ct', although there is no proper hallmark.

Plate 17. This detail of the front of the gold cross shows part of the superbly engraved decoration.

and this done at the right moment does a deal of good. But it is practice and experience, together with man's own discretion, that are the only real ways of teaching one how to bring about good results in this or in anything.'

In workshops where town gas was available the goldsmith used a gas-burner tube fitted to the bench. The piece to be soldered was supported on a hand-held *wig* of fine iron wire (also known as the *devil*) and held up to the flame. A concentrated area of heat was achieved using the blowpipe held in the gas flame whilst the surrounding glow of the wire wig helped to raise the overall temperature.

Casting

In addition to constructing jewellery by soldering together a number of separately formed parts, the goldsmith has always made use of casting techniques. For the more massive items such as buckles or heavy signet rings the sand mould may be used, although intricate work was modelled in wax and cast into gold or silver using the *lost-wax process.* However, the casting of jewellery in precious metal in the eighteenth and nineteenth centuries was rare because of the difficulty of achieving high-quality castings which were also light enough to meet the constraints of the market place. The tendency would have been to model in wax only special pieces for subsequent casting. (The silversmith, however, would have made considerable use of castings for tea-pot spouts, handles and other components for his trade.)

The mass-production use of lost-wax casting developed from applications in dentistry during the 1920s and 1930s. Cast work may be identified from the seam line, which is often visible, or the metal, when viewed through an eyeglass, will exhibit a grainy surface. Tiny spheres, or bubbles of metal, tucked away in corners are clear proof of a lost-wax casting.

Mass-production

During the second half of the nineteenth century advances in the design and construction of machinery brought mass-production to the manufacture of jewellery. Press tools for cutting and shaping thin metal sheet and for decorating surfaces turned the craftsman into a skilled assembly worker, producing thousands of bangles, brooches and lockets in which the sole objective was to combine the maximum volume of metal with the minimum weight of gold. Unfortunately, this philosophy still governs many areas of the trade.

7
The important gemstones

The best gemstones, whether of a scarce or common type, should, when shaped and cut, be more than simply pretty; ideally they should possess an enigmatic quality that draws the eye back to look again and again. Certain stones have always been highly prized because they possess, in varying degrees, three important properties: rarity, beauty and hardness.

Assessing the value of a stone can be a highly subjective business, particularly when dealing with unusual examples. However, some generalisations can be made. The value of a precious stone will rise at a faster rate than the increase in size or weight. For example, a half carat ruby might cost £250, which is a rate of £500 per carat. However, a 2 carat ruby of the same quality could well cost £4,000, which, at £2,000 per carat, is a fourfold increase in price per carat. As an example from 1865, a half carat brilliant diamond had a value of £6 (£12 per carat), whereas a 5 carat stone was valued at £350 (£70 per carat). The larger stone showed a sixfold increase in price per carat.

Similar dramatic increases in price per carat are also influenced by the colour of a stone, where a subtle improvement in shade can prompt an apparently disproportionate rise in cost. One reason for the use in jewellery of fields of small stones (pavé settings, see chapter 10) is that it is a way of achieving good-quality colour at a comparatively low cost. Larger stones to cover the same area would perhaps quadruple the cost for no significant improvement in overall visual effect.

The extent to which a particular gemstone is used in any period may depend on its availability. The sudden popularity of a stone may follow the discovery and exploitation of a new source. For example, the opening up of South African mines after 1870 led to a huge increase in the wearing of diamond jewellery, and also to the wider use of the brilliant, since the losses in cutting were suddenly less important. (The simpler form of the rose-cut diamond is not as wasteful as the brilliant; see figures 34 and 35.) However, during the Boer War the supply of diamonds was restricted so jewellers turned to other stones, notably peridot and opal.

Precious gemstones are sold by weight and the *carat* (0.2 grams) is the standard measure. (Do not confuse this term with the carat as used in expressing the fineness of gold alloys, shown in figure 17.) The carat is divided into 100 points: thus a 20 point diamond would weigh one-fifth (0.2) of a carat. As examples of size, a 0.25 carat diamond brilliant would be 4.1 mm in diameter and a 1 carat diamond 6.5 mm in diameter, although these might well vary according to how they were cut.

Different types of gemstone material do not weigh the same for a given volume. Thus diamond, which has a specific gravity (density) of about 3.5, is lighter than sapphire, with a specific gravity of 4. Therefore a 1 carat ruby would be smaller than a 1 carat diamond, whereas a 1 carat emerald would be considerably bigger.

A widely used indication of the relative hardness of minerals is the *Mohs' hardness scale,* which is a means of classifying materials by listing them in order of their potential both for scratching a softer mineral and being themselves scratched by one that is harder. It is not an accurate system but does offer a guide as to a stone's resistance to wear and therefore its usefulness for jewellery.

The identification of any gem material is fraught with difficulty. Even without the plethora of imitations and synthetics, it is often impossible to establish with absolute certainty the identity of natural stones unless expensive diagnostic equipment is used.

Diamond

The diamond is a supremely hard pure crystalline form of carbon. It frequently occurs naturally as an octahedron (a double pyramid, see figure 33), and it was in this shape, with the plane surfaces polished, that it was first used. Improvements in the cutting greatly enhanced its beauty and encouraged its wider use. The rose cut, in its various forms (figure 34), gives to the diamond a soft lazy fire rather than the spectacular glitter of the modern brilliant (figure 35). Because of the extreme hardness of the stone it will tend to outlast the setting, a feature which helps to identify it. Although diamonds are hard they are not unbreakable: an accidental blow can chip or even shatter a stone, especially if there is a flaw or fault within the material.

Apart from its hardness, the most prized quality of diamond is that of dispersion: its ability to split white light into widely separated bands of colour. It is this feature which gives the stone its characteristic *fire.*

Plate 18. A cluster of rose-cut diamonds in a nineteenth-century white-gold setting, mounted on a modern ring. The stones themselves were possibly cut at an earlier date. The large central diamond is pear-shaped whilst the side stones are very roughly circular. Although they all have different weights and outlines, each one follows the facet layout of the Dutch rose (see figure 34).

Ruby and sapphire

Next in hardness to diamond is *corundum* (aluminium oxide), gem-quality crystals of which are better known as ruby and sapphire. The fact that ruby and sapphire are both corundums was not recognised until about 1800, and before that date they were frequently confused with the less valuable garnet and spinel. Ideally, ruby should be a rich full red with just a hint of blue, and sapphire a strong cornflower blue. If a ruby is pale enough to be pink, it should be called a *pink sapphire*. Corundum occurs as a transparent white crystal and also in a wide range of colours. *White sapphire* does not exhibit the fire (dispersion) of a diamond. The *star sapphire* and *star ruby* show a six-pointed star when viewed beneath a single light source. This effect (asterism) is caused by minute parallel fibres of rutile and is less marked in diffused lighting conditions. Stones in the corundum group have been manufactured synthetically since 1900 and these may well be found in old jewellery (see chapter 8 and figure 30).

Emerald, aquamarine and beryl
Stones in the beryl group have a wide range of colours but the most familiar are the sea-blue *aquamarine* and the rich green of the highly prized *emerald*. The latter is rare and seldom flawless: indeed the term *jardin* (garden) is given to inclusions and they are valued as evidence that the stone is genuine. The characteristic network of faults makes it a fragile gemstone in spite of the hardness. Usually it will have been boiled in oil to improve the clarity. The aquamarine and emerald are often given a rectangular step cut which is also known as the emerald cut (see figure 38).

The gemstone *beryl* may be defined as any member of the beryl group which cannot be classified as an emerald or aquamarine and the colours range from golden yellow through green to orange and red.

Chrysoberyl
The *chrysoberyl* is found in many colours, including the range from yellow to brown. The most valuable forms are the *cat's-eye chrysoberyl* (always cut as a cabochon) and the *alexandrite* (named after Tsar Alexander II), with its fascinating colour change from purple-red to green-blue.

Topaz
Topaz tends towards light delicate shades of blue, pink and, more commonly, yellow. Most highly prized are the pinks and golden sherry colours.

Spinel
Red is the more usual colour for spinel, which also occurs as blue, yellow, pink and orange. There has in the past been much confusion between spinel and ruby, especially since they are often found together, and it was only in about 1830 that they were recognised as different minerals. Since the 1930s good-quality spinel has been widely manufactured.

Garnet

Garnet is a familiar stone in older jewellery, where the commercial grade of orange-brown has, perhaps, given it a bad reputation. There are six different types of garnet, ranging from the fine green of *grossular garnet*, through yellow and orange, to red. Some shades of garnet are very beautiful. In cabochon form it is known as a *carbuncle*. In the past pale garnets were often rose-cut (figure 34) and set with coloured foil behind the flat back in order to improve the colour.

Tourmaline

Green and to a lesser degree pink are probably the most familiar tourmaline colours but it is a gem with a vast range, of which red and emerald green are the more valuable. Most crystals show more than one shade and the cutting may be done to reveal two or more colours in one stone.

Zircon

Known in the past as *jacinth*, zircon is usually white but does have a beautiful blue variation. This is commonly obtained by heating transparent material and the result is easily confused with aquamarine. The yellow-red-brown variety is called *hyacinth*. Zircon's high refractive index and dispersion give it a brilliance and fire approaching that of diamond. Although reasonably hard, it is a brittle stone.

The quartz group

The gemstones so far discussed have been dealt with in descending order of Mohs' hardness, from 10 for diamond, 9 for the corundums, 7½ to 8 for beryl and so on to approximately 7 for zircon. This figure of 7 is significant because it is the hardness of quartz, an abrasive dust which is common to our environment and which will scratch and damage anything softer than itself. Thus gemstones of hardness 6 and below, such as opal, malachite and peridot, are especially vulnerable, particularly when set in a ring, because they will tend to lose their polish and in time develop an unattractive matt finish.

Many gemstones are varieties of quartz, of which the most precious is flawless, deep purple *amethyst*. Clear yellow quartz is known as *citrine*, whilst the brown variety is *smoky quartz*. These can both be confused with the more valuable (and harder) topaz. Smoky quartz from Scotland is called *cairngorm*. *Rose quartz* is a pink form of quartz, though it is rarely a clear transparent crystal suitable for faceting. Colourless crystal is known as *rock crystal* and in faceted form it has been widely used for costume jewellery although it does not have the brilliance of diamond. The original *rhinestones* were of rock crystal but they are now made of glass.

Aventurine is a green quartz with an iridescence which is caused by tiny inclusions of mica. Yellow *tiger's eye* also depends on inclusions (of fibrous quartz) for its easily recognised appearance. The blue variety of tiger's eye is called *hawk's eye.*

Yet another quartz is *chalcedony,* which comes in many colourful guises. There is the translucent *cornelian,* with a range of shades from flesh tones, through orange, to a brown-red, at which stage it is more accurately referred to as *sard.* The bright green variety is *chrysoprase,* whilst dark green with red spots or flecks is known as *heliotrope* or *bloodstone.* The green inclusions in *moss agate* closely resemble waterweed although the stone often contains areas of red. It is seen to best effect when cut into thin slabs and viewed against the light.

Agate is, correctly, a banded or layered chalcedony which occurs as nodules or geodes. Because of its porosity, the dyeing and staining of agate has been practised for centuries, particularly with dull material. Blues and greens, for instance, are achieved using dyes. Old stones of a good natural colour may well have escaped this treatment.

If the agate has parallel layers of black and white it is called *onyx.* This is used for making cameos by carving the image in the white layer, which is then cut back around the edge to reveal the black background. A variation is *sard* or *sardonyx,* a white and brown layered variety, whilst *cornelian onyx* is white on a red base.

Yet another quartz is *jasper,* also known as *hornstone,* a further variety of chalcedony, with a wide range of colouring and patterns. It may be of spotted, streaked or banded appearance.

A final member of the quartz group, and one with the lowest hardness (5½ to 6½), is *opal,* a delicate stone in both structure and colouring. *Black opal* is the most valuable, though it is seldom actually black, the base colour frequently being dark grey, blue or green. *White opal* has a light or milky-white base. Opal is an unusual gemstone in that it has a non-crystalline structure and is known to shrink slightly and suffer crazing of the surface through loss of water. It is always cut as a cabochon (usually shallow). *Fire opal* is an orange form of opal but without the characteristic iridescent play of colour. *Water opal,* which is pale and almost colourless, is yet another variety. Doublets and triplets are well established composite stones using opal (see figure 31). Because it is comparatively soft, opal found in old jewellery will usually have lost its polish. The belief that wearing opals is tempting fate in some way is of relatively recent origin; in ancient times they were regarded as lucky.

Olivine

The transparent olive-green gemstone known as olivine or *peridot* has a soft delicate appearance and is usually faceted when cut. Also sometimes called *chrysolite*, it found considerable favour in jewellery of the early nineteenth century, then later in the Edwardian period. There are important deposits of this stone on the Island of St John in the Red Sea.

Jade

Jade, also known as *kidney stone,* is a tough, slightly translucent green mineral which, in the 1860s, was proved to occur in two forms, *nephrite* and the more valuable *jadeite.* It is often difficult to differentiate between the two forms, both of which can include black flecks and streaks of green on a cream-coloured

Plate 19. A fine nineteenth-century ring, in gold, set with natural pearls surrounding a turquoise. The outer edge of the setting forms a bezel (the claw effect is decorative) whilst the turquoise and the inner edges of the pearls are gripped by small areas of metal that have been beaded and spread. The shoulders have been deeply modelled by engraving.

base. Nephrite itself is found in a wide range of colours: yellows, reds, browns, white and black, all of which may be improved by the use of dyes.

Haematite and pyrite

Haematite, with its slightly unreal, dark grey metallic lustre, is an ore of iron. It is cut for intaglios and signet ring stones. In the past it was much used in mourning jewellery.

Closely related to haematite is pyrite, a yellow iron ore with a distinctive metallic appearance. It is known as 'fool's gold', and with every justification since there is little chance of confusion because pure gold is almost four times heavier. Pyrite is found in many pieces of old jewellery (and it is still used), in the form of small rose-cut faceted stones which are generally known as *marcasites*.

Moonstone

Moonstone is the most important gemstone in the *feldspar* group. It is usually colourless but may exhibit a cat's eye effect caused by the lamellar structure or, in the more sought-after examples, it contains a delicate blue sheen or bloom. It is always cut as a cabochon and is frequently found in jewellery from the East.

Turquoise

Turquoise, an opaque stone of a characteristic pale blue, has been popular in jewellery of all ages. Clear sky-blue is the most prized although turquoise matrix (turquoise veined with brown, black or grey) is a dramatic and valuable variation from which larger stones are often cut. Because turquoise is porous the colour can be improved by the use of dyes. Unfortunately, the porosity also means that the stone can turn an unpleasant green through the action of cosmetics, perspiration and even soap.

Lapis lazuli

Lapis lazuli, like turquoise, has its own unique colour, which at its best is an intense royal blue. Since the stone is opaque it is always cut in cabochon-related shapes. Tiny flecks or inclusions of iron pyrites are a valued feature. *Sodalite* is of similar, though darker, appearance and can be confused with lapis lazuli.

Malachite

The vivid green of malachite is easy to recognise. It is an ore

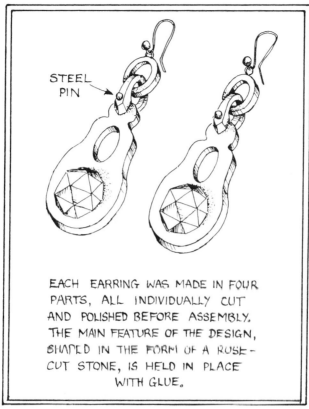

STEEL
PIN

EACH EARRING WAS MADE IN FOUR
PARTS, ALL INDIVIDUALLY CUT
AND POLISHED BEFORE ASSEMBLY.
THE MAIN FEATURE OF THE DESIGN,
SHAPED IN THE FORM OF A ROSE-
CUT STONE, IS HELD IN PLACE
WITH GLUE.

Figure 29. Earrings made from jet: a typical design dating from about 1880.

of copper which exhibits layers or banding. It is opaque and takes a good polish but, being soft (Mohs' hardness 3½ to 4), it also easily loses it.

Organic gem materials

Gem materials of organic origin have always been important in jewellery although confusion is caused by the number of very clever imitations which have been used to simulate the genuine material.

Amber has been the subject of more clever copies than most, some of them useful because they are stronger than the real thing. Amber is a brittle fossilised resin which ranges from pale yellow to a dark red-brown and may be either transparent or opaque. A number of resins may be confused with amber, including *copal*, which is of recent origin and of a lighter colour.

Jet, which used to be mined near Whitby in North Yorkshire, was enormously popular during the second half of the nineteenth century, especially in mourning jewellery. A form of fossilised wood, it is black and may easily be carved, although it is quite brittle. (Figure 29 shows an example.) There were a number of imitations, the most successful of which was a hard black rubber called *vulcanite.* The shiny black glass which was known as *French jet* was probably popular as a material in its own right rather than as an imitation of jet.

Coral has a limited range of colours, usually white, pink, red and black. Because coral develops as a branching skeleton, pieces of large diameter are rare. It is shaped as beads or cabochons, used in the form of small uncut 'twigs' and sometimes made into small carvings. The reds tend to be the most highly prized.

With its complex pattern of growth lines, *elephant ivory* can be easy to identify. However, ivories with different textures also come from the *walrus, hippopotamus* and *narwhal.* Ivory tends to crack and turn yellow with age.

Tortoiseshell is obtained from the hawksbill turtle and was widely used in Victorian jewellery, particularly for piqué work (figure 16). It was shaped by heating and moulding it, as also was *horn,* a less attractive substitute. For many years tortoiseshell has been imitated successfully by plastics.

The marine shells of *abalone,* with their iridescent lustre, are widely used in jewellery, as are the large oyster shells which provide *mother-of-pearl.* Layered shells are also important for the carving of shell cameos.

The *pearl* has, in the twentieth century, been cultured by inserting a bead of mother-of-pearl into the mantle of the oyster and allowing a few layers of nacre to be deposited on the surface. By this means a truly spherical pearl is produced. Totally natural pearls, however, grow in the oyster over many years, starting from a minute speck, and during this process there is invariably some deviation from the perfect sphere. Pearls that have suffered radical deformation are prized as *baroque pearls.* In contrast to the cultured pearl, the natural pearl is a build-up of many layers of nacre. Even to the expert, cultured and natural pearls are indistinguishable without the use of special instruments. Extreme dehydration of a pearl can cause the surface to develop minute cracks. Pearls are normally strung on silk, with knots between them to eliminate damage due to abrasion.

8
Synthetic and imitation stones

The use in jewellery of imitation gemstones is a long established practice, dating from Greek and Roman times, and seldom carried out with any serious intention to deceive. Usually it was (and still is) the only form in which the less wealthy could acquire jewellery which had at least the surface appearance of grandeur.

Paste

Coloured or clear *glass* is the most widely used material for making imitation gems, and these are commonly referred to as paste. Various types of glass are used, including a leaded composition which has a high refractive index and a dispersion equal to that of diamond. One form of this lead glass is known as *strass*. It is, however, very soft, which is the drawback to all pastes since the surfaces soon become scratched and dull. One feature that can help to identify paste is the presence of characteristic swirl lines and minute air bubbles trapped in the glass. Another clue to the identity of the stones may be found in the quality of the setting: for example paste is not usually put into well made, 18 carat gold settings.

Glass can be faceted and polished, using traditional gem-cutting methods, or it may be formed in a mould, with or without subsequent polishing of the facets. Moulded glass can usually be detected by its lack of crispness and the coarsely finished seam line at the girdle of the stone. Often foil is placed behind paste, or the back of the glass itself may be coated with a reflecting surface.

Some of the most desirable pastes are the cameos and intaglios made by James Tassie, and later by William Tassie, in the late eighteenth and early nineteenth centuries. They produced in glass high-quality copies of many famous engraved gems.

Synthetic gems

An imitation gemstone is a fake, an inferior material which is trying to look like a superior one. Since about 1900, however, there has been the added complication of the synthetic gemstone.

A synthetic gem is a duplicate (not an imitation) of the natural material, having the same crystal structure, the same chemical ingredients and the same physical properties. The first successful synthetic gems were rubies which were made in France in 1902

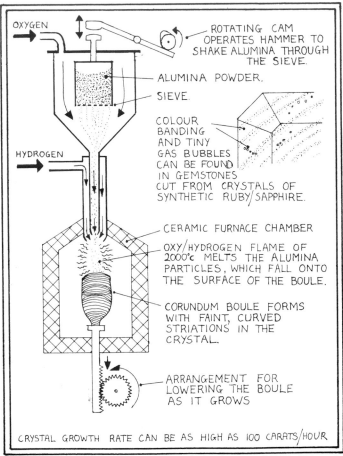

Figure 30. Diagram showing the Verneuil flame fusion furnace of 1904. Although different techniques are now used for growing synthetic corundum (ruby/sapphire), the Verneuil furnace is still in use.

by August Verneuil using the flame fusion process (figure 30). These were followed by sapphires, in a variety of colours. Emerald, spinel and even quartz were soon added to the list of successful synthetics. Since the 1950s there have been others, including diamond, but these are all too recent to concern us here.

Composite gems

Yet another way of producing a convincing result is by making composite gemstones (see figure 31). For instance, the back part (pavilion) of a stone may be made of soft glass whilst the top (crown) is made using a harder material, perhaps garnet. A variation of this is the *soudé emerald*, in which the crown and pavilion are both made from quartz or colourless spinel held together using a green cement. The result is surprisingly good and difficult to detect. Many variations of composite stones have been used with success in jewellery.

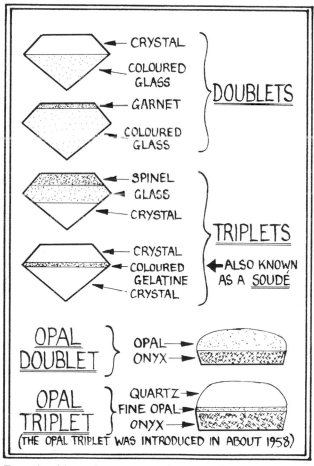

Figure 31. Examples (shown in cross-section) of fabricated gemstones. Doublets and triplets can be surprisingly hard to detect.

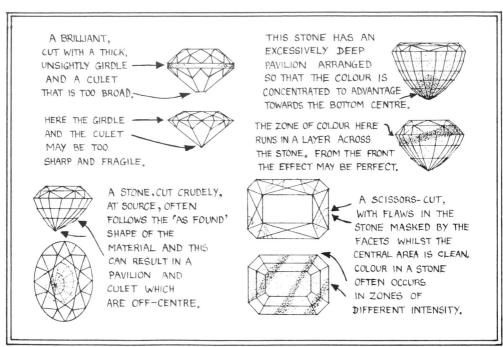

A BRILLIANT, CUT WITH A THICK, UNSIGHTLY GIRDLE AND A CULET THAT IS TOO BROAD.

HERE THE GIRDLE AND THE CULET MAY BE TOO SHARP AND FRAGILE.

A STONE, CUT CRUDELY, AT SOURCE, OFTEN FOLLOWS THE 'AS FOUND' SHAPE OF THE MATERIAL AND THIS CAN RESULT IN A PAVILION AND CULET WHICH ARE OFF-CENTRE.

THIS STONE HAS AN EXCESSIVELY DEEP PAVILION ARRANGED SO THAT THE COLOUR IS CONCENTRATED TO ADVANTAGE TOWARDS THE BOTTOM CENTRE.

THE ZONE OF COLOUR HERE RUNS IN A LAYER ACROSS THE STONE. FROM THE FRONT THE EFFECT MAY BE PERFECT.

A SCISSORS-CUT, WITH FLAWS IN THE STONE MASKED BY THE FACETS WHILST THE CENTRAL AREA IS CLEAN. COLOUR IN A STONE OFTEN OCCURS IN ZONES OF DIFFERENT INTENSITY.

Figure 32. Typical faults in cut gemstones.

Figure 33. Simplified summary of the development of the diamond brilliant cut.

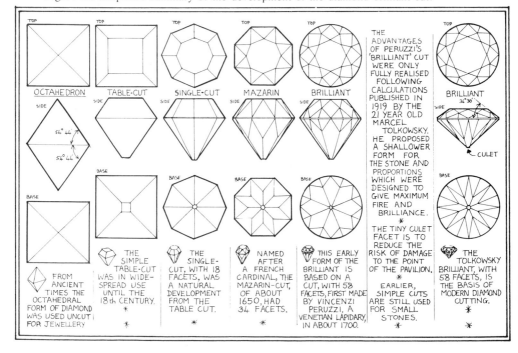

OCTAHEDRON

FROM ANCIENT TIMES THE OCTAHEDRAL FORM OF DIAMOND WAS USED UNCUT FOR JEWELLERY

TABLE-CUT

THE SIMPLE TABLE-CUT WAS IN WIDE-SPREAD USE UNTIL THE 18th CENTURY.
*

SINGLE-CUT

THE SINGLE-CUT, WITH 18 FACETS, WAS A NATURAL DEVELOPMENT FROM THE TABLE CUT.
*

MAZARIN

NAMED AFTER A FRENCH CARDINAL, THE MAZARIN-CUT, OF ABOUT 1650, HAD 34 FACETS.
*

BRILLIANT

THIS EARLY FORM OF THE BRILLIANT IS BASED ON A CUT, WITH 58 FACETS, FIRST MADE BY VINCENZI PERUZZI, A VENETIAN LAPIDARY, IN ABOUT 1700.

THE ADVANTAGES OF PERUZZI'S 'BRILLIANT' CUT WERE ONLY FULLY REALISED FOLLOWING CALCULATIONS PUBLISHED IN 1919 BY THE 21 YEAR OLD MARCEL TOLKOWSKY. HE PROPOSED A SHALLOWER FORM FOR THE STONE AND PROPORTIONS WHICH WERE DESIGNED TO GIVE MAXIMUM FIRE AND BRILLIANCE.
*
THE TINY CULET FACET IS TO REDUCE THE RISK OF DAMAGE TO THE POINT OF THE PAVILION.
*
EARLIER, SIMPLE CUTS ARE STILL USED FOR SMALL STONES.
*

BRILLIANT

THE TOLKOWSKY BRILLIANT, WITH 58 FACETS, IS THE BASIS OF MODERN DIAMOND CUTTING.
*

9
Stone cutting

The cutting and polishing of a gemstone are an attempt to reveal the inherent beauty of the material, which, if it is opaque or slightly translucent, is generally given a smooth rounded *cabochon* shape (figure 40), whereas the more transparent material is usually cut with polished *facets,* arranged to make the most of the colour, refractive index and dispersion of that particular gem (figure 37 for example).

As stone cutting techniques have been steadily improved with the aid of science and mathematics, so the natural properties of the gem material have been better exploited.

Stones cut in the West tend to be more precise than those shaped by the lapidary at source (often crudely and with primitive equipment), because there has always been a demand by jewellery manufacturers for stones to be cut to accurate dimensions, as this speeds up quantity production. However, greed frequently influences the shape of a stone. For instance, a cutter will be loath to remove surplus material to arrive at an ideal form if his payment for the final product is to be related directly to its carat weight.

Clever cutting can be a way of disguising unattractive features (see figure 32). For example, a thin colour can be enhanced by adding depth to the lower part (pavilion) of the stone, whilst a shallow cut can bring out the best in a piece of excessively dark material. Often stones are cut with disfiguring flaws cunningly situated at the edges or so arranged that the best colour is at the centre. Flaws reduce the value of a stone but may also be an indication that it is of natural origin. In the trade there is a tendency to avoid the pejorative term 'flaw' when describing a fault in a stone, the less accurate word 'inclusion' being used instead.

The cutting and polishing of diamonds has long been a separate skill from that of the other precious and semi-precious stones, whilst the shaping of agate, jasper and similar materials, normally cut as cabochons, has also been the province of specialists.

In ancient times all gemstones, except diamonds, were cut as cabochons, so the full beauty of the material usually remained hidden. The cutting and engraving of intaglios was, however, an art form which reached astonishing levels of sophistication. In the ancient world, the Greeks made the finest engraved gems.

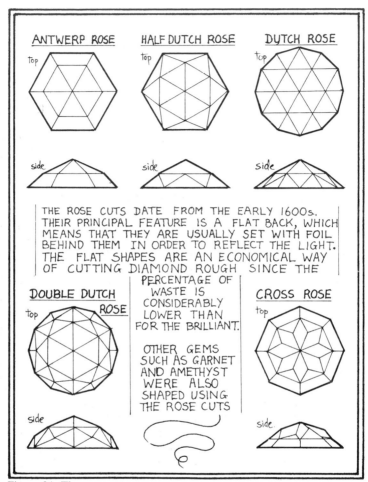

Figure 34. The rose cuts.

Early attempts at faceting stones in order to produce an improved effect would have been a matter of trial and error and much labour. It is interesting to study the Cheapside Hoard, which was found in 1912 in London and was possibly the stock-in-trade of a jeweller. Dated to about 1600, the collection included many fancy-cut stones (one of which, an octagon, is illustrated in figure 39) and also cabochon-cut garnets and emeralds. The diamonds, however, were in the form of the

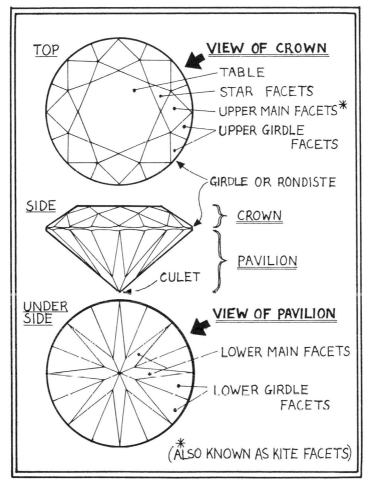

Figure 35. The brilliant form of cutting with its 58 facets.

simple table cut because the rose cut had yet to come fully into use and the brilliant was not developed until about 1700 (figure 33).

It is highly probable that the hardness of diamond was one of the reasons for the delay (when compared to the coloured stones) in developing a suitable cut. The only way to shape a diamond is to rub it with another diamond, relying on the fact that the hardness varies slightly according to the angle of individual

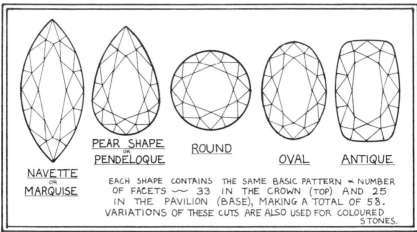

Figure 36. The modern brilliant cut of 1912, with its specific angles and proportions, has been adapted for a wide variety of shapes of diamond.

Figure 37. The Ceylon, scissors and French cuts.

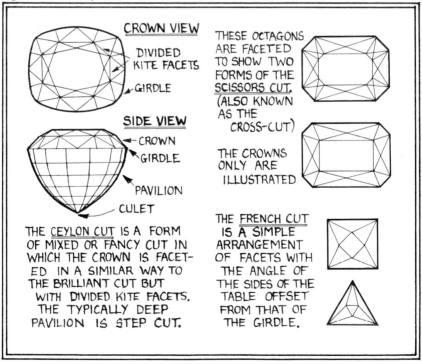

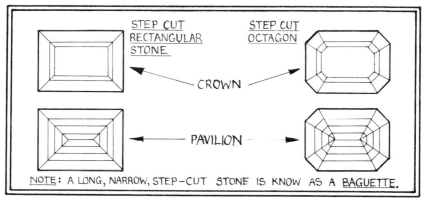

Figure 38. The step or emerald cut.

Figure 39. Three examples of mixed cuts.

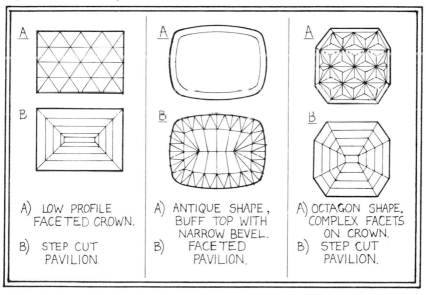

crystals within the structure of the material. The diamond powder generated is used for polishing. Diamonds can also be split along cleavage planes and this technique has been widely used to speed the process.

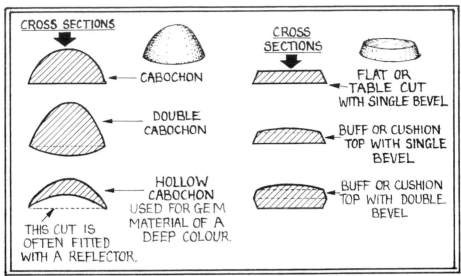

Figure 40. Variations of the cabochon cut.

Figure 41. Different forms of the collet setting in which the stone is held in place by a metal collar or bezel.

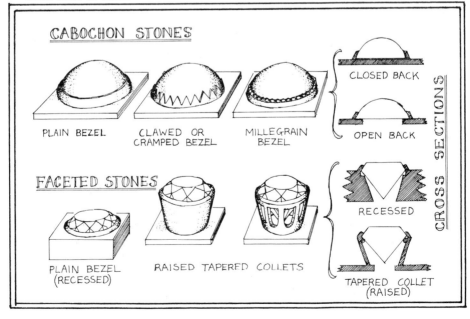

10
Gemstone settings

The major feature in most jewellery, and often the most valuable ingredient, is the gemstone. This must therefore be held firmly on to the jewel by some mechanical means that is aesthetically pleasing yet also very secure. Except in cheap or fashion jewellery and for fixing pearls, adhesives are never used. Stone setting is one of the most demanding of the jeweller's skills, in which he must contrive, in some unobtrusive way, to form an arrangement to grip the stone firmly, but without risk of damage to what might well be a valuable and fragile gem. Emerald and opal are examples of stones that require considerable care when setting.

The collet or bezel

The collet or bezel is one of the most secure settings and is particularly appropriate for cabochon stones and cameos, although it is also used for faceted stones where an extra tight grip is essential (figure 41). The setting is made by constructing a rim or collar of plain or decorated metal which just fits around the base of the cabochon (or girdle if setting a faceted stone). The metal rim is pressed and burnished down around the stone to provide a tight and even grip. Often, on sterling silver jewellery, the bezel is made from fine silver because it is more easily pressed into place. When setting a fragile gem, the metal bezel is sometimes serrated to give the effect of a row of tiny claws. A similar effect can be produced if a millegrain wheel has been used in order to form a series of tiny beads around the top edge of the collet (see figure 41).

The collet is probably the earliest form of setting and it lends itself to use with high-carat golds which are soft enough to burnish over the gem. It is the type of setting which is found in medieval jewellery, where it is often, rather dramatically, embellished with claws.

The gypsy setting and Roman setting

The gypsy setting, which is usually used for rings, is a method of recessing a stone with angled sides (such as a cabochon) into the surface of the jewellery and holding it in place by hammering the surrounding metal tightly around it, as shown in figure 42. The object is to have the stone projecting from the surface in a

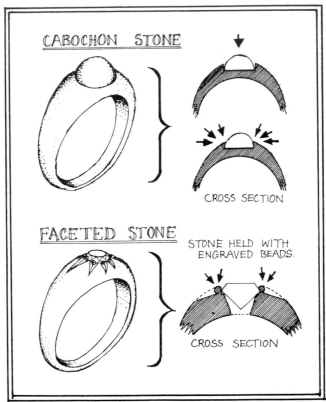

Figure 42. Typical gypsy settings in which the girdle of the stone is recessed into the surface and gripped using the surrounding metal. The rings illustrated would be referred to as gypsy rings.

very clean and neat way, leaving no evidence of the actual setting.

The *gypsy ring* uses this form of setting but often, instead of cabochons, it makes use of faceted stones. These are recessed slightly so that the tables are almost level with the surface of the metal and then they are held in place using beaded settings (see figure 47 for details). This creates a decorative star around the stone where the metal is chiselled up to form the beads. In essence, a gypsy setting is one in which the stones are set into, rather than on, the surface of the metal.

A variation of the gypsy setting is the *Roman setting,* which is frequently used for holding flat stones, such as intaglio seals (figure 43). Again a recess is created, into which the stone fits very accurately. A groove is then scooped out of the metal around the stone, but slightly away from it, using a graver. One wall of this groove is then driven sideways against the angled edge of the stone to hold it firmly in place.

The claw setting

The familiar claw setting, which is most frequently used in conjunction with transparent faceted stones, is intended to raise up and display the gemstone whilst keeping the surrounding metal to a minimum (figure 44). Usually at least four claws are used to grip the stone, with a maximum of eight for small settings. For many years claw settings have been available to manufacturers as ready-made components (stampings) but it is always worth looking carefully at an old piece of jewellery to see if the claws have been sawn and filed by hand. It is usually the more expensive items that receive such care and attention.

There are many special names that have been given to the various designs of claw setting but none is reliable for identifica-

Figure 43. The Roman setting is used principally for mounting intaglios or seal stones in signet rings and fobs.

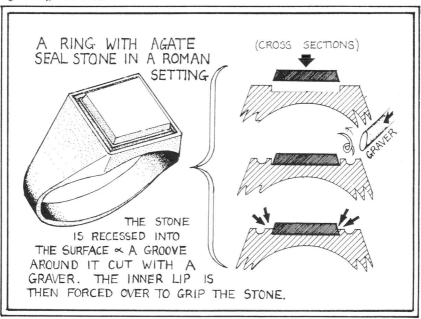

A RING WITH AGATE SEAL STONE IN A ROMAN SETTING

(CROSS SECTIONS)

GRAVER

THE STONE IS RECESSED INTO THE SURFACE & A GROOVE AROUND IT CUT WITH A GRAVER. THE INNER LIP IS THEN FORCED OVER TO GRIP THE STONE.

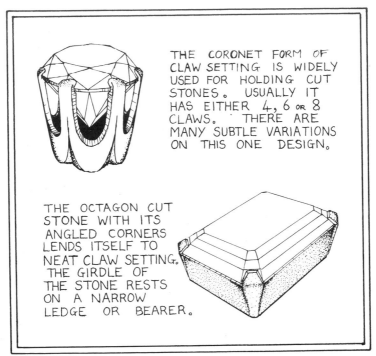

THE CORONET FORM OF CLAW SETTING IS WIDELY USED FOR HOLDING CUT STONES. USUALLY IT HAS EITHER 4, 6 OR 8 CLAWS. THERE ARE MANY SUBTLE VARIATIONS ON THIS ONE DESIGN.

THE OCTAGON CUT STONE WITH ITS ANGLED CORNERS LENDS ITSELF TO NEAT CLAW SETTING. THE GIRDLE OF THE STONE RESTS ON A NARROW LEDGE OR BEARER.

Figure 44. The claw setting.

Figure 45. An illusion setting with a bead-set stone.

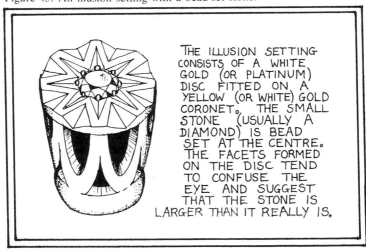

THE ILLUSION SETTING CONSISTS OF A WHITE GOLD (OR PLATINUM) DISC FITTED ON A YELLOW (OR WHITE) GOLD CORONET. THE SMALL STONE (USUALLY A DIAMOND) IS BEAD SET AT THE CENTRE. THE FACETS FORMED ON THE DISC TEND TO CONFUSE THE EYE AND SUGGEST THAT THE STONE IS LARGER THAN IT REALLY IS.

tion. Such terms as *crown, coronet* and *rex* have been used and they all refer to the obvious crown-like appearance of the setting. They are also known in America as prong settings, and the six-prong variety is called a *Tiffany setting* because it was introduced by Charles Tiffany in 1886. In France they are *chatons* or *heads*.

Very often the claw setting will be of white gold on a yellow gold ring, or it may be 18 carat on a 9 carat ring, or platinum on an 18 carat ring. Many combinations are used, either because a white stone demands white metal claws, or because a softer, less springy metal is required. Sometimes just the tips of the claws will be made in platinum.

A cunning arrangement that is used in jewellery is the *illusion setting* (figure 45). This is a claw setting with a flat, white-gold disc soldered on to the prongs. Into the centre of the disc a small stone (often a very small diamond) is set, using a beaded setting. The result is that the facets of the cut star surrounding it become confused with the facets of the tiny stone, which as a result gives the illusion of being bigger than it really is.

Stones with a large circumference are claw-set by using *gallery strip,* a stamped-out row of prongs which can be folded round to form any size of setting (figure 46).

An elaborate type of multiple claw setting is the *cluster,* in which the centre stone is held in prongs whilst the side stones are set at a lower level, each with one or two claws on the outside edge but with the inner part of the girdles held in slots cut into the base of the centre stone prongs.

The beaded setting

Related to the claw setting is the beaded setting (figure 47) which is sometimes also known as *thread and grain*. It is widely

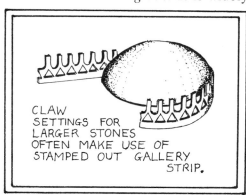

CLAW SETTINGS FOR LARGER STONES OFTEN MAKE USE OF STAMPED OUT GALLERY STRIP.

Figure 46. A large claw setting.

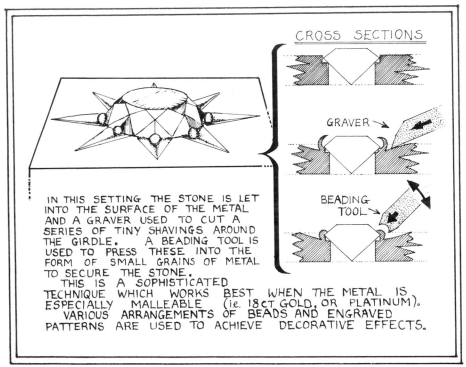

CROSS SECTIONS

GRAVER →

BEADING TOOL →

IN THIS SETTING THE STONE IS LET INTO THE SURFACE OF THE METAL AND A GRAVER USED TO CUT A SERIES OF TINY SHAVINGS AROUND THE GIRDLE. A BEADING TOOL IS USED TO PRESS THESE INTO THE FORM OF SMALL GRAINS OF METAL TO SECURE THE STONE.
 THIS IS A SOPHISTICATED TECHNIQUE WHICH WORKS BEST WHEN THE METAL IS ESPECIALLY MALLEABLE (ie. 18CT GOLD, OR PLATINUM).
 VARIOUS ARRANGEMENTS OF BEADS AND ENGRAVED PATTERNS ARE USED TO ACHIEVE DECORATIVE EFFECTS.

Figure 47. This type of beaded (or thread and grain) setting is sometimes also known as a star setting.

used for securing small stones or where a massed or *pavé* (French, paved) effect is wanted. The stone is recessed slightly into the surface of the metal and held in place by a number of tiny beads or grains, which are formed from chiselled-up threads or chips of metal. A beading or graining tool, which has a concave tip, is pressed on to the threads to re-shape them into beads, which are pushed against and slightly above the girdle of the stone. The bright chiselled cuts which are made in the metal are carefully positioned to form a star-shaped decorative feature (see also figure 4). A frequently used beaded setting, without the star effect, is the *carré* setting, which is shown in figure 48.

The beaded settings are best carried out in the more malleable, higher-carat gold alloys. Often the setting area itself is in platinum to provide a white surround for diamonds although silver was sometimes used for the settings on old jewellery made in gold.

Figure 48. The carré setting.

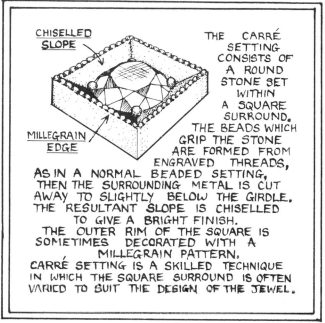

CHISELLED SLOPE

MILLEGRAIN EDGE

THE CARRÉ SETTING CONSISTS OF A ROUND STONE SET WITHIN A SQUARE SURROUND. THE BEADS WHICH GRIP THE STONE ARE FORMED FROM ENGRAVED THREADS, AS IN A NORMAL BEADED SETTING, THEN THE SURROUNDING METAL IS CUT AWAY TO SLIGHTLY BELOW THE GIRDLE. THE RESULTANT SLOPE IS CHISELLED TO GIVE A BRIGHT FINISH. THE OUTER RIM OF THE SQUARE IS SOMETIMES DECORATED WITH A MILLEGRAIN PATTERN. CARRÉ SETTING IS A SKILLED TECHNIQUE IN WHICH THE SQUARE SURROUND IS OFTEN VARIED TO SUIT THE DESIGN OF THE JEWEL.

Plate 20. Detail of the central section of a hinged bracelet in 9 carat gold. The stones (sapphires and pearls) are secured using beaded carré settings (see figure 48). Here all the beads have been recut, indicating that the stones were removed and reset, probably to enable repairs to be made. Made in about 1900, the bracelet is a hollow structure with added decoration.

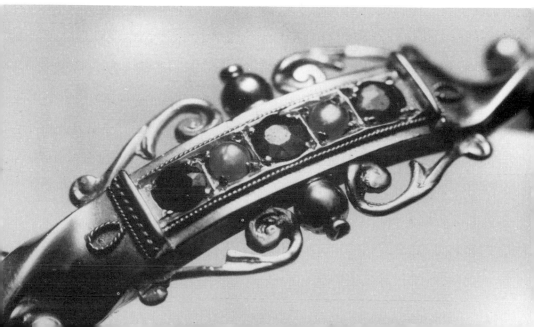

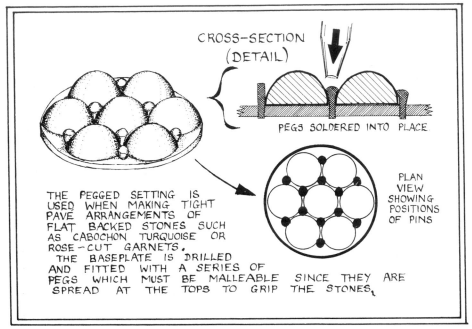

CROSS-SECTION
(DETAIL)

PEGS SOLDERED INTO PLACE

THE PEGGED SETTING IS
USED WHEN MAKING TIGHT
PAVÉ ARRANGEMENTS OF
FLAT BACKED STONES SUCH
AS CABOCHON TURQUOISE OR
ROSE-CUT GARNETS.
  THE BASEPLATE IS DRILLED
AND FITTED WITH A SERIES OF
PEGS WHICH MUST BE MALLEABLE SINCE THEY ARE
SPREAD AT THE TOPS TO GRIP THE STONES.

PLAN
VIEW
SHOWING
POSITIONS
OF PINS

Figure 49. The pegged setting.

Figure 50. The channel setting.

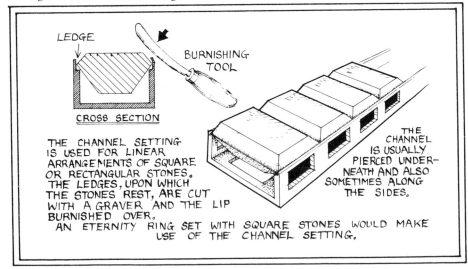

LEDGE

BURNISHING
TOOL

CROSS SECTION

THE CHANNEL SETTING
IS USED FOR LINEAR
ARRANGEMENTS OF SQUARE
OR RECTANGULAR STONES.
THE LEDGES, UPON WHICH
THE STONES REST, ARE CUT
WITH A GRAVER AND THE LIP
BURNISHED OVER.
  AN ETERNITY RING SET WITH SQUARE STONES WOULD MAKE
USE OF THE CHANNEL SETTING.

THE
CHANNEL
IS USUALLY
PIERCED UNDER-
NEATH AND ALSO
SOMETIMES ALONG
THE SIDES.

In forming a pavé setting the stones are arranged very close together and the beads to secure them are carefully raised by chiselling up metal in the tiny gaps between them.

Other settings

Another way of setting stones when a massed effect is wanted is to use a *pegged setting* (figure 49). This technique allows a closer grouping of the stones (they can be touching each other) although generally it is only suitable for cabochon or rose-cut shapes, both of which have angled sides and are flat at the back. In this setting the stones are arranged on a flat metal surface and tiny pegs or pins are fixed in the spaces between them. The tops of these pegs are then pushed down so that they thicken and spread slightly, gripping the surrounding stones. If this method is used well, it can be almost invisible.

Pavé effects are also achieved using the *burred setting*. Here

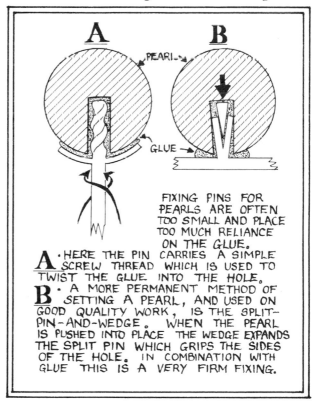

Figure 51.
Pearl-fixing methods.

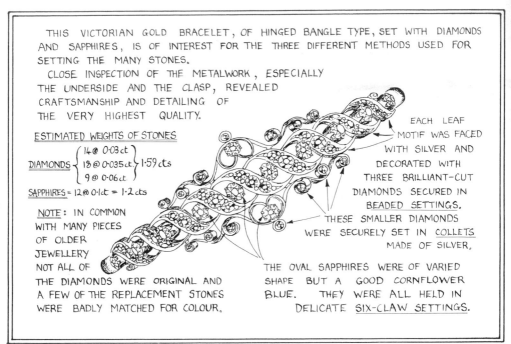

THIS VICTORIAN GOLD BRACELET, OF HINGED BANGLE TYPE, SET WITH DIAMONDS AND SAPPHIRES, IS OF INTEREST FOR THE THREE DIFFERENT METHODS USED FOR SETTING THE MANY STONES.

CLOSE INSPECTION OF THE METALWORK, ESPECIALLY THE UNDERSIDE AND THE CLASP, REVEALED CRAFTSMANSHIP AND DETAILING OF THE VERY HIGHEST QUALITY.

ESTIMATED WEIGHTS OF STONES

DIAMONDS $\begin{cases} 14 @ 0.03\,ct \\ 18 @ 0.035\,ct \\ 9 @ 0.06\,ct \end{cases}$ 1.59 cts

SAPPHIRES = 12 @ 0.1ct = 1.2 cts

NOTE: IN COMMON WITH MANY PIECES OF OLDER JEWELLERY NOT ALL OF THE DIAMONDS WERE ORIGINAL AND A FEW OF THE REPLACEMENT STONES WERE BADLY MATCHED FOR COLOUR.

EACH LEAF MOTIF WAS FACED WITH SILVER AND DECORATED WITH THREE BRILLIANT-CUT DIAMONDS SECURED IN BEADED SETTINGS.

THESE SMALLER DIAMONDS WERE SECURELY SET IN COLLETS MADE OF SILVER.

THE OVAL SAPPHIRES WERE OF VARIED SHAPE BUT A GOOD CORNFLOWER BLUE. THEY WERE ALL HELD IN DELICATE SIX-CLAW SETTINGS.

Figure 52. A Victorian bracelet analysed.

the gems are positioned in tight-fitting chiselled-out recesses and the burrs formed around the edges are pushed over to grip the stones.

The *channel setting* is a means of securing a row of square or baguette stones, the edges of the channel being folded over slightly to grip the girdle of the stones, but usually on two sides only (figure 50). This setting allows the gems to be butted up to each other so that the effect is continuous. The method would be used, for example, to secure square stones in an eternity ring.

Faceted gemstones with a table, girdle and pavilion (see figure 35 for definitions) are usually set so that the back is open and accessible. This is done mainly to allow the rear surfaces to be cleaned and not necessarily to allow light to enter the stone from the back. There are a few faceted stones which benefit from being open in this way but a well cut stone, which is viewed from the front, uses light which also enters from the front. However, it is important to keep the rear facets of any stone, including a

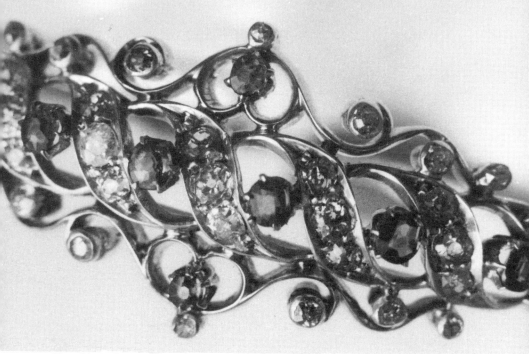

Plate 21. A detailed view of the sapphire and diamond Victorian bracelet illustrated in figure 52.

Plate 22. Rear view of the sapphire and diamond bracelet showing the well made structure.

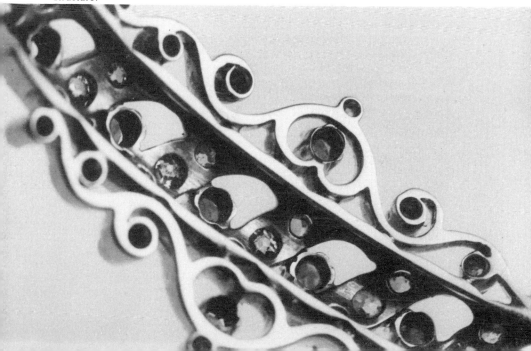

diamond, free from dirt and grease since these have a marked effect on the optical properties.

Translucent stones cut with a flat back, such as cabochon moonstone and garnet or rose-cut diamond, which are held in a setting which is closed at the back, will often have foil inserted behind them. This can either be white foil to reflect light or coloured foil to tint the stone. Enhancing the colour of a stone in this way would today be highly dubious or even illegal practice, but the Victorians seemed to experience no qualms in the matter; very pale garnets could be brought up to a wonderful red with the aid of a tiny piece of coloured foil.

If the back of a stone setting is left open it is referred to as à jour.

As mentioned before, in general the quality of a setting is an indication of the quality of the stone. A cheap stamped-out setting would not be used for a valuable stone, just as a finely made gold setting would normally not be wasted on a worthless piece of paste.

A close examination of an old setting can sometimes reveal whether or not the stone is the original because un-setting and re-setting can seldom be done without some visible damage and disturbance. This applies to bezels and particularly to beaded settings.

Pearls are normally glued on to a peg or pin which carries a tiny spiral groove (figure 51). This is used to twist glue (pearl cement) into the hole in the pearl and it also helps to stop the pin sliding out. A wedge setting is used for very valuable pearls.

STERLING SILVER
(MARKED IN ENGLAND)

STERLING SILVER
(MARKED IN SCOTLAND)

Figure 53. Marks used to indicate the sterling silver standard on British items assayed before 1975. The Irish (Dublin) mark for silver is a crowned harp.

11
Hallmarks

The British hallmark is a well established feature on almost all new jewellery in gold, silver and, since 1975, platinum which is offered for sale in Great Britain. Not only does this cover goods made in Great Britain, but even imported items, with a few exceptions, must be submitted for assay and marking before they can be sold. However, the hallmarking of jewellery has in the past been sporadic and many pieces, especially smaller ones, were never assayed.

The assay and stamping of silver wares were instituted in 1300 by a statute of Edward I, making it the oldest form of quality control still in use in the world.

Usually the hallmark has four component punch marks, which give the following information: the initials or mark of the manufacturer; the type of metal and its standard of purity; the identity of the assay office; and the year in which the piece was assayed.

The *maker's mark*, also known as the *sponsor's mark*, is usually the initials of the goldsmith or the manufacturing company responsible for the work. In some cases it is the mark of the retailer who has sponsored the work. The maker's mark must be registered with the assay office and is an integral part of the assay mark itself.

The *identity of the metal* is marked in various ways. English sterling silver is indicated by a lion passant (figure 53) but there are no numbers to show that it is the 925 standard of purity. There are other marks for silver items of Scottish and foreign manufacture, and there is a different mark for Britannia silver (958 standard), though this softer alloy was never intended for the manufacture of jewellery.

Gold, however, has since 1975 been marked with a crown which is accompanied by numbers to indicate the standard of purity in parts per thousand, but it was not always so simple. In the early nineteenth century (actually since 1798) only two official hallmark standards were recognised for gold jewellery, namely 18 carat and 22 carat. This situation persisted until 1854, when the lower standards of 9, 12 and 15 carat were introduced. For almost eighty years these five gold assay standards were used; then in 1932 a simplification took place when the 12 and 15 carat were dropped and replaced by the 14 carat standard. (Figure 54

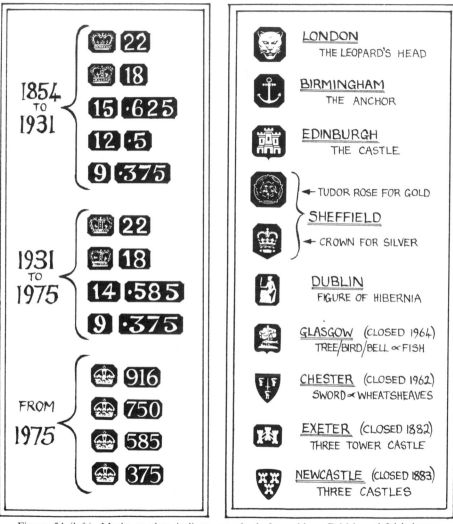

Figure 54 (left). Marks used to indicate standards for gold on British and Irish items assayed after 1854.

Figure 55 (right). The assay office marks indicating the town in which the item was hallmarked.

shows details of these changes.)

In these earlier assay marks (before 1975) it will be seen that the crown was not used for the lower standards (those other than 18 and 22 carat), the gold content being shown both as a carat number (parts per 24) and as a decimal (parts per one).

The *assay office mark* indicates that the work was assayed at one of the following towns: London, Birmingham, Edinburgh, Sheffield, Dublin, Chester (closed 1962), Glasgow (closed 1964), Newcastle (closed 1883) and Exeter (closed 1882) (see figure 55). This *town mark*, as it is sometimes called, gives a clue to the area in which a manufacturer worked but it is not a wholly reliable guide since there is nothing to stop a jeweller working at Land's End from sending his pieces to Sheffield for assay provided his mark is registered there.

The *year of assay* was indicated within the hallmark by a letter of the alphabet which was different for each assay office, and it changed at various times of the year according to which assay office did the marking. Thus London changed in May, Birmingham and Sheffield in July, and Edinburgh in October. Since 1975, however, all the assay offices have been using the same synchronised alphabets and the change of letter is made at the end of the year. When an alphabet sequence reaches Z a new typeface is adopted and marks start once more at A.

Many marks use distinctive shield-like surrounds and these can help with identification. However, they are not entirely reliable. Often different surrounds were used for gold and silver although the date letter remained the same.

The additional use of the sovereign's head in the assay marks between 1784 and 1890 was to show that duty had been paid.

Imported goods submitted for assay after 1867 were given an F mark in addition to the normal marks, but in 1904, to avoid confusing the F mark with date letters, modified carat standard marks and a special series of symbols unique to each assay office were brought into use (figures 56 and 57).

The hallmarking of platinum, to a standard of 950, dates only from 1975. Before that year the metal was simply given a mark such as PLAT by the manufacturer.

Other marks

The hallmarking of jewellery, unlike larger items of gold and silverware, seems to have been the exception rather than the rule in the past and many pieces were either not marked at all or were given simple unofficial indications as to the quality of the metal,

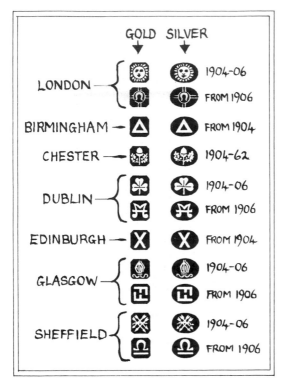

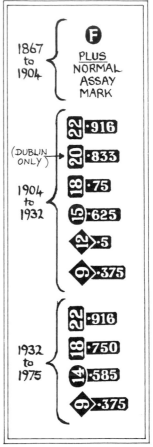

Figure 56 (left). The assay office town marks used on imported items since 1904 are totally different from those used when marking goods of home manufacture.

Figure 57 (right). Marks used to indicate standards of gold on imported items between 1867 and 1975.

such as 15 K or 9 KT or 9 CT. These do not constitute hallmarks and they should always be treated with a degree of scepticism.

The use of K or *k* instead of C or CT for carat is an indication that jewellery is of other than British manufacture since the term 'karat' is a specifically American spelling of the word.

The term GOLD FILLED is also of American origin and dates from about 1870. The expression is misleading because it means that the object is made from a base metal with, on both sides, a gold surface only. It does not mean that the object is filled with gold!

Plate 23. The pleasure of owning good jewellery is enhanced if it comes complete with the original fitted box.

Similarly the mark ROLLED GOLD or RG indicates that the object is made of a base metal with a thin surface layer of gold alloy, normally on one side only. Sometimes the ROLLED GOLD is qualified by a mark to show which carat gold has been used.

Informal marks for silver include STERLING, SIL or simply a number such as *800, 850* or *935,* to indicate parts of silver per thousand.

Punch marks which give the country of origin are often difficult to decipher since they are seldom as clear and consistent as those of the British assay system. However, it is well worth studying some of the continental European marks because a familiarity with the more important ones can help to make sense of the most obscure devices.

12
Hints for the collector

As with any collection, the cardinal rules are to buy only what you like, then if you pay too much it does not matter quite so much, and always try to collect pieces that are in good condition or that can be repaired at a reasonable cost. The satisfactory repair of worn settings and claws can be expensive. The incomplete or damaged pieces in any collection can become an irritation to any serious collector.

Approach with great caution the matter of cleaning or restoring any piece of jewellery, and if in doubt do nothing. The proper repair of old jewellery is a job for the specialist and too many pieces have been ruined by the use of such things as lead solder or a pair of clumsy pliers.

Always inspect old or antique pieces with an eyeglass before purchase and insist on a receipt which details the identity of the metal and particularly the stones. Beware of inaccurate or misleading descriptions of stones, for example 'cape ruby' (garnet) and 'Manchurian jade' (soapstone). Finally, be wary of the term 'antique': it does not always mean what it suggests.

13
Places to visit

Intending visitors are advised to find out the times and days of opening before making a special journey.

Ashmolean Museum of Art and Archaeology, Beaumont Street, Oxford OXI 2PH. Telephone: 0865 278000.
Birmingham Museum and Art Gallery, Chamberlain Square, Birmingham, West Midlands B3 3DH. Telephone: 021-235 2834.
British Museum, Great Russell Street, London WC1B 3DG. Telephone: 01-636 1555.
Geological Museum, Exhibition Road, South Kensington, London SW7 2DE. Telephone: 01-938 8765. An outstanding collection of gemstones.
Museum of London, London Wall, London EC2Y 5HN. Telephone: 01-600 3699.
Victoria and Albert Museum, Cromwell Road, South Kensington, London SW7 2RL. Telephone: 01-938 8500.

14
Further reading

Becker, Vivienne. *Antique and Twentieth Century Jewellery.* NAG Press, second edition, 1987.
Bly, John. *Discovering Hallmarks on English Silver.* Shire, 1986. Contains a list of date marks which apply to gold and silver.
Clifford, Anne. *Cut Steel and Berlin Iron Jewellery.* Adams and Dean, 1971.
Evans, Joan. *A History of Jewellery 1100-1870.* Faber, 1953.
Muller, Helen. *Jet Jewellery and Ornaments.* Shire, 1980.
Schumann, Walter. *Gemstones of the World.* NAG Press, 1977.

Index

Page numbers in italic refer to illustrations.